Acknowledgments

I would like to take the opportunity to thank all those who have contributed in some way to this position paper.

Recognition should first be given to the core team of the Banking Advisory Group who issued this document:

- Valérie Aubert, KBL European Private Bankers SA, Luxembourg
- Iglika Evtimova, Bulgarian National Bank, Bulgaria
- Florence Fradin, BNP Paribas, France
- Piotr Kosmala, AIG Bank, Poland
- Kim-Andrée Potvin, BNP Paribas, Luxembourg
- Roberto Russo, Poste Italiane, Italy
- Michael Schiwietz, Hypovereinsbank, Germany
- Elizabeth Styf, Riksgälden, Sweden.

I would also like to thank:

- all the internal auditors who were unfailingly ready to help us, especially those who responded in detail to our survey documents and questionnaire.
- IIA Inc who gave us permission to enrich our document with CBOK data.
- Louis Vaurs, CEO of the French Internal Audit Institute (IFACI), Claude Cargou, Past President of IFACI and member of the ECIIA Board, Mauro di Gennaro, President of ECIIA, and Phil Tarling, member of the ECIIA Board, who helped us with this position paper and who gave me their assistance.
- Mathieu Ponsot and Grégoire Corcos, BNP Paribas, France, whose contribution was essential to the publication of this paper.

Finally, I would like to thank Danièle Nouy, Secretary General of the French Banking Commission (former Secretary General of the Basel Committee on Banking Supervision and former Chair of the Committee of European Banking Supervisors) for her foreword. Her words highlight the convergence between the approaches of the European supervisory framework and the work of internal auditing. This support is an encouragement to the Banking Advisory Group to pursue its action in the direction of building a more advanced European banking internal audit function.

Patrice Josnin
Chairman of the Banking Advisory Group
Deputy Head of BNP Paribas Inspection Générale

Foreword

The ECIIA position paper, *Overview of Banking Internal Auditing in Europe*, makes an important contribution – particularly in the context of the current financial turmoil – to the development of a common European approach to internal auditing in the banking sector. The need for more professionalism and for the strengthening of the internal audit function is high on the list of lessons to be learned from the current crisis and the recommendations made by the ECIIA will be extremely helpful in addressing potential weaknesses and preventing abuses.

The method used by the ECIIA has consisted of studying the internal auditing regulations of several European countries and analysing the practice of selected banking groups, so laying the foundations for a 'code of best practice' for internal auditors. This is groundbreaking work on the part of the banking industry. It will be extremely useful, supplementing the work that has already been accomplished by international standard setters, notably the Basel Committee; with its paper on *Enhancing corporate governance for banking organisations*. I am very glad to be associated with this promising project.

The ECIIA's comprehensive overview of internal auditing at European banks reveals that the efforts of regulators and supervisors to deliver a consistent, efficient supervisory framework in Europe – in particular, through the Lamfalussy process – are being mirrored in the field of internal auditing. Internal auditing practices are converging to a significant extent (although more work is needed to achieve further convergence). Convergence in internal auditing practice will clearly help supervisors – and in particular the home supervisors of cross-border banking groups – to ensure that all activities and all risks, world-wide, are managed appropriately.

As the BAG wisely emphasises, there is no single good (and simple) approach to defining and designing a "sound" internal auditing system. Internal auditing structures and practices must be tailored to the activities and structure of each banking entity, and must be reviewed and updated periodically. Nevertheless, a number of objective elements can be identified which are crucial to the sound operation of internal audit, whatever the organisation, the size, or the business line.
We expect these elements to be implemented in every internal auditing system, in order to achieve the level of efficiency and safety that is needed in the banking system.

The proficiency of the internal auditors is certainly one of the key elements. Auditors need excellent professional expertise and skills, and appropriate incentives, in order to adapt to the rapidly changing financial environment. Another key element is the independence of the auditors, which should be reinforced by the implementation of the 8th Directive. The introduction of mandatory audit committees for banks will help as well.

The dialogue which ECIIA has initiated with the internal auditing profession in Europe is totally in line with the discussions underway for some time past, regarding modifications to the European regulatory and supervisory framework. Better cooperation between national (home and host) supervisors, and enhanced convergence in their supervisory practice, are needed in order to fill potential supervisory gaps and address the cross-border activities of European banking groups. These supervisory improvements are gradually being introduced and should continue to take place in the Lamfalussy process of integration of the national supervisors. The contribution of the ECIIA promises similar progress in the field of auditing. Just as supervisors are developing a common European supervisory culture, the ECIIA's work on best practice for European auditors will help develop a European culture of internal auditing.

Danièle Nouy
Secretary General of the French Banking Commission
former Secretary General of the Basel Committee on Banking Supervision – BCBS
former Chair of the Committee of European Banking Supervisors – CEBS

Contents

Figures and Tables

Introduction

Until 2004, the European banking market was, with a few exceptions, concentrated in national markets. But the last four years have seen this situation change, with many European cross-border operations and the emergence of larger institutions. Examples of this development are:

- the takeover of the British bank Abbey National by the Spanish group Santander in July 2004
- the purchase of the German bank HVB by Italian Unicredit in November 2005
- the purchase of the Italian bank Antoneveneta by the Dutch bank ABN Amro in January 2006
- the purchase of BNL (Italy) by BNP PARIBAS in February 2006
- the purchase of ABN Amro by the European consortium Royal Bank of Scotland, Fortis (Belgium/Netherlands) and Santander (Spain) in October 2007
- the purchase of CCR (France) by UBS (Switzerland) the same month
- the purchase of Antoneveneta (Santander) by Monte dei Paschi (Italy) in November 2007
- the purchase of Dresdner by Commerzbank (Germany) in September 2008.

At the end of 2006, the banking market in the EU consisted of 8,441 credit institutions and 212,000 bank branches with total assets of €36,820 billion. Of these, 45 were cross border banking groups.

The banking sector is the backbone of any economy within its interconnections to social and political systems. Banks play an important role of intermediation in the economic system, by making financial resources allocation efficient. When providing credit, collecting and replacing savings and operating in the financial markets, the banks are necessarily exposed to risks.
Indeed, the failure of a banking institution has the potential to impact the entire economic system, if the so called "domino effect" occurs.

Moreover, as shown by several recent cases of fraud, any weakness in the internal control system of a bank can generate significant losses. Before the Société Générale fraud early 2008, a similar case had already occurred in February 1995 at the former British investment bank, Barings, leading to a loss of $1.2 billion and the demise of the institution as an independent entity.

In this context and in order to guarantee the stability of the entire system, two key factors deserve particular attention:

- The effectiveness of European regulation in the banking industry: the European institutions have embarked on the implementation of a single market in financial services, albeit within competitive and multi regulatory constraints, which ensure that the process will take time to be completed.
- The deployment by the banking organisations, at the request of the national regulators, of sound risk management, of an effective internal control framework and of an efficient internal audit function.

The aim of this document is to give internal auditors an overview of European banking regulations and of their impacts on the internal audit function. It also aims at giving a practical overview of the organisation and role of internal audit in the Europe banking sector, with a particular emphasis on the competencies and skills required for internal audit.

This paper highlights topics that are currently the focus of European and national attention, such as cooperation between national supervisors (seen by some as the first step towards European banking supervision), Corporate Governance, the role of the Audit Committee and the positioning of Internal Audit within the Organisation.

Most of these topics are presently under active discussions in various national and European committees and commissions. This paper therefore also reflects the position of the European Banking Advisory Group towards these important internal control issues.

In this *Overview of Banking Internal Auditing* in Europe, we have sought in our thinking to be comprehensive, and to answer the following questions:

- What are the specific banking regulations for internal control? (Part 1).
- How is internal control organised in the banks and who are the main proponents? (Part 2).
- What is the role and scope of Internal Audit in banking?
- How is this function positioned within banks and what is its organisation?
- Does the audit function represent an attractive career opportunity for a young or aspiring executive and what specific skills and competencies should an auditor have? (Part 3).

It should be noted that this position paper has not sought views from employers. It does however reflect the opinion of the members of the Banking Advisory Group of ECIIA.

This position paper was written using the results of a survey (see questionnaire in Appendix 1) completed by internal auditors (BAG survey respondents), from 18 European countries (see Appendix 2). The European banking data was extracted from the CBOK Survey[1] of the IIA (see Appendix 3, CBOK Survey respondents). These data were used to complete the findings.

---

[1] In 2006, The IIA Research Foundation conducted a comprehensive, global survey known by its abbreviation as the CBOK ("Common Body of Knowledge") Survey, devoted to the practice of Internal Audit around the world. IIA received about 12,000 responses. The survey set out to determine the knowledge and skills possessed by internal auditors, the duties performed, the structure of internal audit organisations, and the types of industry practicing internal audit.

Thirteen Banking Advisory Group Positions on Key Internal Audit Issues

1. Regulatory environment
The need is for the increasing convergence of national regulations and beyond for the promotion of European regulation.

2. Banking supervision
The need is to switch from a national to a European logic, suited to the cross-border scope of the European banking groups.

3. Organisation of and actors in Internal Control
The need is to ensure that the Internal Control system encompasses different lines of defence and that Internal Audit is sufficiently prepared for and committed to performing the final assessment within the framework of the various control bodies.

4. Positioning of Internal Audit
The need is to position the Internal Audit function at the highest level within the Organisation and to ensure that the function has a strong link with the Board or the Audit Committee, particularly when reporting directly to the Chief Executive Officer.

5. Audit Committee
The need is to reinforce the link between the Audit Committee (an essential body of Corporate Governance) and Internal Audit, enabling the Chief Audit Executive to meet alone and as often as necessary with the Chair of the Audit Committee.

6. Structure
The need is to adopt the most efficient organisation (centralised / decentralised; specialised auditors / generalists…) to suit the size of the Bank and the level of complexity of its activity.

7. Scope and role of Internal Audit
The need is to assume a primary security role, yet when conducting a consulting assignment, ensure that it is excluded from the scope of responsibility of the Chief Audit Executive.

8. Risk approach or control approach?

The need is for strong commitment to a well-balanced Risk approach, and to a Control approach when establishing the audit plan, particularly as recent incidents show that adverse events may occur expectedly.

9. Is the Internal Auditor an *ex post* controller?

The need is not only for an *ex post* but also an *ex ante* auditor role; which requires giving internal audit the tools and resources to assume both roles.

10. Internal Audit and Corporate Governance

The need is to include Governance issues within the scope of audit, whilst excluding specific areas to allow their assessment by external reviewers (Corporate Governance bodies of the parent company).

11. Is the outsourcing of the Internal Audit function a contradiction in terms?

The outsourcing of parts of Internal Audit may be acceptable, but in specified circumstances only.

12. Quality Assurance Review

The Quality Assurance Review program should combine self-assessment and external review in order to maintain high quality standards and determine the added value of Internal Audit.

13. Profile and career path of Auditors

By optimising the efficiency of the internal audit team, by employing a combination of experienced professionals and young executives, and making Internal Audit a "school" of management preparing for larger operational responsibilities, Internal Audit can become an attractive function offering adequate incentives for career development.

Part 1

Banking Internal Control Regulatory Environment

Part 1   Banking Internal Control Regulatory Environment

1.1.   Banking Internal Control Regulations and Supervisors[2]

1.1.1.   International Standards: the Basel Committee

The Basel Committee on Banking Supervision is a forum to promote discussion and policy analysis among Central Banks and within the international financial community. It deals with supervisory questions and banking Internal Control issues. Its members come from 13 countries, namely Belgium, Canada, France, Germany, Italy, Japan, Luxembourg, the Netherlands, Spain, Sweden, Switzerland, the United Kingdom and the United States. The countries of the Basel Committee are represented by their Central Bank or by the authority with formal responsibility for the supervision of banking.

The objective of the Basel Committee is to improve the quality of banking supervision by exchanging information on national supervisory issues, approaches and techniques and promoting a common understanding. The Basel Committee also develops guidelines and supervisory Standards, such as the international capital adequacy Standards ("Basel II").

With respect to Internal Control and Internal Audit, some of the Committee's main publications are:
- *Core principles for effective banking supervision*, September 1997 (updated in October 2006)
- *Core principles methodology*, October 1999 (updated in October 2006)
- *Internal Audit in banks and the supervisor's relationship with auditors*, August 2001 (updated in August 2002), where the Basel Committee recognises the Internal Audit professional Standards of the Institute of Internal Auditors (IIA) (see Appendix 6)
- *Customer due diligence for banks*, October 2001

---

[2]   Main bodies involved in and rules applicable to banking internal control.

- *The relationship between banking supervisors and the bank's external auditors,* January 2002
- *General guide to account opening and customer identification,* February 2003
- *KYC (Know Your Customer) Risk Management,* October 2004
- *Compliance and the compliance function in banks,* April 2005
- *Enhancing corporate governance for banking organisations,* February 2006
- *Basel II International Convergence of Capital Measurement and Capital Standards,* a revised Framework June 2006.

The Basel Committee does not possess any formal supranational supervisory authority, and its conclusions do not have legal force *per se*. It formulates Standards for supervisory directives and recommends best practice, expecting that the national authorities will apply them in their national regulations, either directly or via European Directives. These then become mandatory when their contents are placed in a normative frame:
- either in Community law
- or in National law (in legislation *stricto sensu* and also the enactments of authorities having a regulatory power (and/or power of accreditation)

In addition, the Basel Committee is accepted as a setter of "good market practice" in the international financial community. Its recommendations provide sound guidelines for an effective system of internal control and auditing. Various institutes adopt the Committee's recommendations as internal Standards without necessarily waiting for their adaptation to national law.

1.1.2. European "Regulations": EBC and CEBS

EBC (European Banking Committee)
EBC is run by the European Commission (EC). The Committee fulfils both a "comitology" function (a European Commission word meaning Committee work) and advisory functions. It assists the EC in the adoption or implementation of European Union (EU) Directives. EBC is made up of representatives from the 27 EU countries and is chaired by a representative of the EC. EBC is a so-called Level 2 Committee under the four levels of the Lamfalussy approach (Figure 1, page 24).

CEBS (Committee of European Banking Supervisors)
CEBS is comprised of the Banking Supervisors and the Central Banks of the 27 European Union countries (namely Austria, Belgium, Bulgaria, Cyprus, Czech Republic, Denmark, Estonia, Finland, France, Germany, Greece, Hungary, Ireland, Italy, Latvia, Lithuania, Luxembourg, Malta, Netherlands, Poland, Portugal, Romania, Slovakia, Slovenia, Spain, Sweden and United Kingdom).

The other countries of EEA (European Economic Area), Iceland, Liechtenstein and Norway, as well as the European Commission and ESCB (Banking Supervision Committee), are observers at meetings of CEBS.

CEBS enhances supervisory co-operation, including the exchange of information and acts in an advisory capacity to the European Commission when it comes to the implementation of banking regulations. It also contributes to the consistency of implementation of Community Directives and to the convergence of Member States' supervisory practice through practical guidelines issued in papers written jointly by member countries.

The European Banking Committee has a consultative function on behalf of the EC in regard to the elaboration of Level 1 texts, and a regulation function ("comitology") for the EC in the exercise of its executive powers at Level 2.

In the European context, these two committees represent a first step towards a supranational European banking supervision.

Adaptation process of the European enactments to local regulations

The Community Directives, proposed by the EC and adopted by the Council of Ministers of the EU and the European Parliament, are not directly applicable on a national level in the 27 Member States of the EU but must be transposed into the domestic law of each Member State. This adaptation is generally made via national laws and application decrees. Every Member State is free to choose the particular form and means of implementation, but must implement the European Directive within a given time frame (18 months on average).

A particular procedure of "comitology", known as the Lamfalussy procedure,[3] aims at accelerating the adoption of the Community enactments affecting the banking sector, and at guaranteeing their appropriate implementation at the national level. This process allows the more elaborate drafting of instructions and regulations for practical purposes, since the details of implementation are prepared after consultation with the main bodies or organisations concerned. A specialised committee will elaborate these details with the regulators of the Member States. These details are then approved by a representative of the finance sector of each Member State. The process takes place on four levels, which are:

1. the adoption of the legislation framework (Directive framework)
2. the adoption of measures of execution (Directive or application regulation)
3. the adaptation to domestic law
4. the control of law enforcement

---

[3]   The so-called Lamfalussy procedure was established by the Committee under the chairman of that name made up of highly respected personalities, in a report of 15 February 2001 on the regulation of the European securities markets, being extended in 2002 to the banking and insurance sectors.

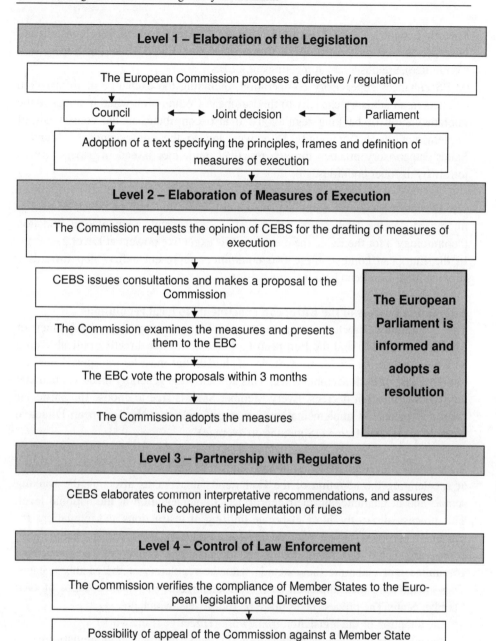

Figure 1: Lamfalussy scheme for banking regulation (Source: French Banking Federation).

The Lamfalussy procedure defines the concepts of **Home and Host supervisors**:

- A home supervisor is responsible for the supervision of banking groups on a consolidated basis at the home location of the headquarters.
- A host supervisor is responsible for the supervision of banking operations in its jurisdiction. Each host supervisor should bring to the home supervisor the necessary information needed for it to complete its mission.

At time of publication, the Lamfalussy procedure is currently under revision, with the aim of reinforcing the role of the Level 3 committees in order to ensure a better convergence of supervisory activities. In this context, the "comply or explain" principle for the Member States is to be applied.

The Level 3 committees are the following:

- CESR (Committee of European Securities Regulators) is an independent committee made up of members attached to national Securities Regulators.
- CEIOPS: (Committee of European Insurance and Occupational Pensions Supervisors) is made up of members attached to the national Insurance controllers.
- CEBS (Committee of European Banking Supervisors) is comprised of the Banking Supervisors and the Central Banks of the 27 European Union countries, namely Austria, Belgium, Bulgaria, Cyprus, Czech Republic, Denmark, Estonia, Finland, France, Germany, Greece, Hungary, Ireland, Italy, Latvia, Lithuania, Luxembourg, Malta, Netherlands, Poland, Portugal, Romania, Slovakia, Slovenia, Spain, Sweden and United Kingdom.

1.1.3. National Regulations

At present, regulations and banking supervision are essentially national, i.e. each European country has its own rules, regulations and supervisory authorities.

The national supervisor, i.e. the local "Banking Commission", is in charge of control and supervision of all banks located in a given country.

The main supervisory goals are to

- maintain the national banking system's strength and stability even under adverse circumstances.
- ensure that each institute duly obeys all legal and regulatory requirements.
- examine the financial and risk situation of particular banks as well as the adequacy of their framework of internal controls, compliance and internal auditing.

The supervisor's objectives overlap in general, and the main principles of banking regulation are similar. However, there is some divergence with respect to national characteristics and their level of detail.

When it comes to Internal Control, all BAG Survey respondents commented that respective national regulations exist and that the national supervisors perform the prudential monitoring of the implementation of those regulations (see Table 1).
In particular in France and Luxembourg, banks are required annually to remit to their supervisors a report on their internal control system.

For example, the French regulation (CRBF/ CCLRF[4] 97–02, Article 42) states:
"At least once a year, credit institutions shall draw up a report on the conditions under which internal control is conducted. This report shall include:
a) *an inventory of the investigations carried out in the field in a manner precisely identifying the main lessons to be drawn, and particularly the principal shortcomings observed, as well as the follow-up to the corrective action taken*
b) *a description of the significant changes made in the field of internal control during the period under review, in particular so as to take into account developments in activities and risks*
c) *a description of the application of the procedures set up for new activities*
d) *a section relating to the internal control of foreign branches*
e) *a presentation of the main initiatives planned in the field of internal control.*
Credit institutions and financial holding companies supervised on a consolidated basis shall also at least once a year draw up a report on the conditions under which internal control is carried out at group level."

The relevant Luxembourg CSSF[5] regulation requires each bank to prepare *"a situation report from the senior management of the bank on the internal control: the purpose of the report is to give a general assessment of the internal control, of the insufficiencies, of the corrective measures and of the follow-up of those measures"*.

Finally, in almost all the countries represented in our survey, there was also a national Banking Federation. The role of these federations is to represent the interests of banks and to be loci of exchanges of view and discussion. Generally, banking organisations are actually required to join the national federation. For instance, the Turkish Banking Law N° 5411 Article 79 states that *"Deposit Banks and development and investment Banks are obliged to become members of the Bank Association of Turkey, which is a professional organisation having the status of public legal person, and to do so within one month of the date of receipt of their operating permission"*.

---

[4] CRBF: Comité de la Réglementation Bancaire et Financière. CCLRF: Comité Consultatif de la Législation et de la Réglementation Financières.
[5] CSSF: Commission de Surveillance du Secteur Financier.

Country	Regulation	Supervisor of the regulation	Web site
Belgium	Circular D 97/4	Belgium Banking Commission	www.cbfa.be
Bulgaria	Ordinance 10	Bank of Bulgaria	www.bnb.bg
Czech Republic	Banking law	Czech National Bank	www.our bank.cz
Denmark	Executive order on auditing	Danish Financial Supervisory Authority	www.dfsa.dk
Finland	Corporate Governance and Business Activity	Finn Financial Supervision Authority	www.rahoitustarkastus.fi
France	CRBF 97/02	Commission bancaire	www.banque-france.fr
Germany	KWG (German Banking Act); Minimum Requirements for the Management of Risk (MaRisk)	Bundesamt für Finanzdienstleistungsaufsicht	www.bafin.de
Italy	Testo unico finanza	CONSOB	www.consob.it
	Testo unico leggi materia bancaria e creditizia	Banca d'Italia	www.consob.it www.bancaditalia.it
	Istruzioni di Vigilanza Titolo IV Capitolo XI	Banca d'Italia	www.bancaditalia.it
Luxembourg	Circulars 98/143 and 96/126	CSSF	www.cssf.lu
Netherlands	Act on Financial Supervision	The Netherlands Authority for the Financial Markets	www.afm.nl
Poland	Banking Act	Bank of Poland	www.nbp.pl
Portugal	Bank of Portugal Regulations	Bank of Portugal	www.bportugal.pt
Slovenia	Banking Act	Bank of Slovenia	www.bsi.si
Sweden	Finansinspection directives	Finansinspection (Swedish FSA)	www.fi.se
Switzerland	Circular 06/6	Swiss Federal Banking Commission	www.ebk.admin.ch
Turkey	Turkish Banking Law (numbered 5411)	Banking Regulation and Supervision Agency	www.bddk.org.tr (Turkish)
	Regulation on Banks' internal systems		http://www.bddk.org.tr/Default_EN.aspx (English)
United Kingdom / Ireland	Section 6.2	Financial Supervision Authority of the UK	www.fsa.gov.uk

Table 1: Summary of the regulations and supervisors cited by the BAG Survey respondents.

1.2.   Will the Current Crisis Hasten European Supervision?

Twenty years after the Single European Act (1987) which has taken the financial system towards a real although very partial harmonisation, national banking supervision still widely prevails.

Juxtaposition of national regulations presents a number of deficiencies notably:
- dispersion of prudential data: cross border banking organisations encounter difficulties in obtaining a consolidated vision of their risks
- no legal and procedural European framework to intervene and coordinate rapidly when a bank faces difficulties in more than one countries of the Union
- too much scattered information and too many participants to make the rapid decisions required in a crisis situation

Although the majority of countries are not in a hurry to promote the convergence of regulation and, still less, to set up a supra national supervisory organisation with true powers, a European approach to banking supervision has significantly progressed in the last 10 years.

The CEBS (Committee of European Banking Supervisors), CEIOPS (Committee of European Insurance and Occupational Pensions Supervisors) and CESR (Committee of European Securities Regulator) are precursors of cross-border supervision. However, they do not have the whole required legitimacy to play the role of a central European supervisor. In a pragmatic way, dialogue does take place, notably through the regular meetings involving bodies such as the CESR or ESC (The European Securities Committee). In the current market place, the needs of the markets are a powerful incentive to go faster in this direction.

But how and to what extent should this European supervision be structured?

There are three main schools of thought:
1. a single European supervision system, identified as the position of Italy (Padoa-Schioppa[6])
2. retention of independence and national supervision, identified as the position of the UK, Germany and the new members of the Union
3. a median position in favour of strong cooperation between national supervisory bodies, identified as the position of the Netherlands and France

---

[6]   President of "Notre Europe," Mr Padoa-Schioppa was Italy's Minister of Economy and Finance from May 2006 to May 2008. He is a Past President of an IMF Committee, and former member of the Executive Committee of the ECB (European Central Bank).

At the ECOFIN meeting held in Nice (France) in September 2008, one of these options should have been chosen. Given the amount of cross-border mergers the European banking industry experienced in the last few years, the nationally focussed supervisory approach appears obsolete. A more consistent supranational regulatory framework and the strengthening of the power of the Level 3 Committees would appear to be necessary to provide the credit institutions and banking groups with coherent regulations and duties throughout all the countries they act in.

To overcome the risk of an over-fragmented supervisory approach, the Basel Committee requires the supervision of global banking groups on a consolidated basis, in order to assess in its entirety the solvency and the liquidity of a group.

Although the establishment of a supranational European supervisor seems utopian given the current level of political European integration, more intense collaboration of the national supervisors is deemed necessary at the operational level.

The perception of the authors of this paper is that in the context of a political framework for European banking supervision, national supervisors must have a wider compass. As we can see, Supervisors and Internal Auditors share a common goal which is to obtain a truly comprehensive view of the risks and risk exposures of European banks.

Banking Advisory Group Position on the Regulatory Environment of the Banking Internal Control

The BAG members consider that formal regulatory requirements regarding Internal Control and the internal audit function in banking institutions are to a large extent converging across European national regulations, and are based upon similar principles and standards. Any differences relate to national characteristics and their levels of detail.

With respect to consistent banking supervision however, the necessity of which arises from the broader reach of cross-border banking groups as well as from the systemic risks inherent in the global financial system, more harmonisation is still deemed necessary.

Although cooperation is in evidence in terms of setting standards, (i.e. through CEBS, CEIOPS and CESR), harmonised and potentially unified operational banking supervision, although just beginning, is still some way off in the current European political framework.

The creation of a supranational supervisor or at the very least, more cooperation between national supervisors (in various forms) is an ongoing process.

In sum, the Banking Advisory Group considers that it is important to switch from national to a European supervisory logic, suited to the cross-border scope of the European banking groups.

Part 2

Banking Internal Control Framework

Part 2   Banking Internal Control Framework

2.1.   BAG Definition of Banking Internal Control

There is no single definition of Banking Internal Control.

According to the COSO[7] definition, *"Internal Control is a process conceived to provide reasonable assurance regarding the accomplishment of objectives. Specifically, it helps achieve objectives relating to the reliability of financial reporting, compliance with laws and regulations, and the effectiveness and efficiency of operations"*.

The IIA defines "control" as *"any action taken by management, the board, and other parties to manage risk and increase the likelihood that established objectives and goals will be achieved. Management plans, organizes, and directs the performance of sufficient actions to provide reasonable assurance that objectives and goals will be achieved"*.

The definitions given by the BAG Survey respondents, notably by the Polish respondent, give some indication of what banking internal control may be in practice: *"Banking Internal Control can be defined as a process [...] designed to provide a reasonable assurance regarding the achievement of objectives in the following categories:*
– effective, efficient and secure business operations
– safe custody of assets, both own and those entrusted
– integrity, exclusivity and completeness of business and financial data and reporting
– compliance to applicable laws and regulations including internal plans, procedures and general policies."

---

[7]   COSO: Committee of Sponsoring Organizations of the Treadway Commission. This American committee wrote "Internal Control – Integrated Framework" in 1992 which is one of the internal control frameworks most frequently in view as a benchmark.

2.2. Organisation of the Banking Internal Control Framework and Main Actors

In the words of seven BAG Survey respondents, the banking Internal Control framework is made up of three lines of defence which can be split into Permanent and Periodic Control.

2.2.1. Permanent Control

The main parties involved in Permanent Control are operational staff, their management and specialised functions.

– **Operational staff** (first line of defence): Internal auditors highlighted in their questionnaire that Banking Internal Control constituted an integral part of each employee's work. In their opinion; the following elements were required to comply with sound principles of internal control, including for example:
  - "Segregation of Duties" meaning that no single individual should have control over two or more phases of an operation.
  - "Four eyes principle" meaning that all business decisions and transactions need to be reviewed by two different persons.

– **Management** (second line of defence), which monitors and supervises Internal Control.
– With the strengthening of controls, specific functions (the second line of defence) have been set up in the last few years. The two main functions of the second line of defence, according to the majority of the banking internal auditor respondents, are **Compliance** and **Risk Management**:
  - Compliance is conformity and adherence to policies, plans, procedures, laws, regulations, contracts, or other requirements.
  - Risk Management is dedicated to the control and reduction of risk to acceptable levels according to the appetite for risk defined by executive management.

In some countries, such as Luxembourg, compliance and risk management functions were identified as a specific line of defence (third line) and internal auditing as the fourth and final line of defence.

2.2.2. Periodic Control

The assessment of the effectiveness and efficiency of the system of Permanent Control is carried out by the internal audit function[8], this being the so called Periodic Control (third or fourth line of defence, see section 2.2.1.).
"The Internal Audit is an integral part of the internal control system of banks and its role is to support management in the process of assessment of the internal control system." (Bulgarian BAG Survey respondent)

Its final role is to be *"responsible for evaluating how well the first and second lines of defence perform their control duties"*. (Sweden BAG Survey respondent)
In France, the Periodic Control is usually called "Inspection Générale" and can be organised in two ways: either the Inspection Générale is the internal audit function, or it constitutes the ultimate line of defence (the fourth one).

It is interesting to highlight that almost all of the surveyed banking internal auditors referred to the IIA definition to explain the internal auditing role in a banking organisations. This we believe demonstrates the uniqueness of the international community of Internal Auditors, characterised by adhesion to a consistent viewpoint.
The IIA defines internal auditing as *"an independent, objective assurance and consulting activity designed to add value and improve an organization's operations. It helps an organization accomplish its objectives by bringing a systematic, disciplined approach to evaluate and improve the effectiveness of risk management, control, and governance processes"*.

A significant number of the respondents to the questionnaire spoke about the Internal Audit Professional Standards. *"The work of internal audit is carried out in accordance with International Standards for the professional practice of internal auditing issued by the Institute of Internal Auditors."* (Finn BAG Survey respondent)

This is not surprising, as the compliance with the IIA Standards is recommended by some national regulations (e.g. Circular 06/6 of the Swiss Federal Banking Commission) and international texts (e.g. Basel Committee).

---

[8]   The role of Internal Audit is defined in section 3.5.

2.2.3. Corporate Governance Bodies: Executive Management and Board

According to many of the BAG Survey respondents, the efficiency of the Internal Control system of their banks came under the responsibility of the corporate governance bodies, the Executive management and/or the Board (Board of Directors or Supervisory Board)[9].

In most European Banks, the Executive management is responsible for the implementation, the assessment and the monitoring of the banking internal control system under the supervision of the Board.

"The Bank's Supervisory Board and Management Board have the ultimate responsibility for ensuring that senior management establishes and maintains an adequate and effective system of internal controls, a measurement system for assessing the various risks of the bank's activities, and appropriate methods for monitoring compliance with laws, regulations, supervisory and internal policies.
The Supervisory Board supervises the implementation of the internal controls and assesses their adequacy and effectiveness. The Audit Committee monitors this on behalf of the Supervisory Board." (Polish BAG Survey respondent)

Like Poland and Finland, some countries indicated the existence of an Audit Committee (a committee of the Board) which performed attentive and regular supervision of the internal control system.

In order to fulfil its responsibilities, the Audit Committee should
– receive reports from all the control bodies (internal and external),
– actively challenge the information reported to it in order to ensure the adequate management of risk.
In the case of highly risk-laden situations and fraud, the parties involved should alert the Audit Committee, as well as Executive management.

The recently adopted European 8th Directive makes the existence of an Audit Committee mandatory for listed companies and public interest entities (including banks). The national transpositions of this Directive should have been completed by the end of June 2008. The enactment formally defines the duties of the Audit Committee as *"the monitoring of the elaboration process of the financial information, the monitoring of the efficiency of the internal control systems, the internal audit, if necessary, and the risk management of the company"*.

---

[9]   A Board is an organisation's governance body, including for example the Board of directors, the supervisory Board, head of an agency or legislative body, or Board of governors, or any other designated body of the organisation, including the Audit Committee, to whom the chief audit executive may functionally report. (Source: IIA).

2.2.4. Internal Control and Internal Auditing

As indicated by the IIA Standards, internal auditing should assess the strength of the internal control system. This role is reinforced by the banking regulations; which in most cases set up a dual system of Permanent and Periodic Control (see notably French Banking regulation CRBF/ CCLRF 97–02).

As mentioned above, banking internal control involves several components; including compliance, accounting control, risk control, quality control and operational control. Each of these has a precise role to play. However, the more components there are, the greater the risk of switching roles. This can lead to a confused organization, including not only expensive overlaps but also loopholes. The temptation is then to merge the control functions while looking for interactions between them.

In this context, the role of internal auditing is to ensure that each control function stays within its boundaries and that no loophole exists in the control system.
As recommended by the World Bank[10], *"internal auditing should ensure that no other bodies perform duties that are within the scope of the activities that are assigned to audit"*.

Internal auditing should also ensure that the interactions between all the control functions are optimized. It should give a reasonable assurance of the efficiency of the internal control system as a whole and of each of its parts and recommend, if needed, measures to reinforce the system.

In this context, internal auditing is a key player in Corporate Governance, as is shown in the graph on Figure 2 (page 38).

---

[10] Strengthening Governance in the banking sector: World Bank Review Methodology, October 2007.

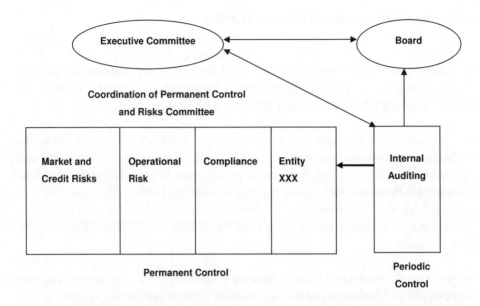

Figure 2: Position of Internal Auditing regarding the Internal Control and Corporate governance bodies.

2.2.5. Assessments of Banking Internal Control

2.2.5.1. Assessment of the Internal Control by External Bodies

The banking Internal Control system is assessed by two other bodies that are outside the organisation itself and provide independent feedback on internal controls. *"Two additional lines of defence are included in the model, the external auditors and the regulators."* (Swiss BAG Survey respondent)

– **Regulators**

As indicated in Part 1, the regulators require that the banking organisations implement an internal control system which is efficient and adapted to the nature and the volume of their activities, their size and the risks to which the banks are exposed. The regulators monitor the bank's internal control system, via the internal control report sent each year by the banking organisation, if required. They can also monitor by performing ad-hoc reviews that can be termed audits.

– **External auditors**

External auditors are audit professionals who perform audits on the financial statements.

The role of the external auditors is to present an unbiased and independent evaluation of the bank's financial statements. Normally, external auditors also review the bank's IT control procedures and investigate any material issues raised by inquiries from regulatory authorities. In some countries, such as Luxembourg, the external auditors already assess the quality and the effectiveness of the internal audit activities, although most of the time the conclusions of these assessments (if any) remain unofficial.

2.2.5.2. Assessment of the Periodic Control (Standard 1300)

As part of the Internal Control framework, Internal Audit should be assessed.

Even if not required by the European regulators, the Quality Assurance Reviews (QAR) can be a good means of maintaining standards of high quality and assessing the value added of the internal audit function. Indeed, the purpose of QARs is not only to check the internal audit function's compliance to the standards of the profession, but more importantly to verify the internal auditors' value added to the organisation. QAR can also be an opportunity to identify areas for further improvement. In some countries, where there is evidence of high quality standards in application, QAR may have the potential to provide additional value to the Organisation, by reducing the frequency and level of external audits.

Thus, the evaluation of the maturity level of the internal audit function within the bank may throw more light on its actual ability to cope with the demanding regulatory framework of the European banking sector.

QAR of the internal audit activity may be performed in a number of ways:
– **Full external review** performed solely by persons outside the organisation, for example, a consulting firm.
– **Peer review:** three internal audit organisations reviewing each other, although this is not an option if commercially sensitive information is to be protected.
– IIA France (IFACI) has developed **an internal audit certification**, inspired by the ISO 9000 Standard. The bank has to reach a standard consistent with the award of a certificate, every three years and each year subsequently, has to maintain it through a follow-up process.
– **Self assessment with independent review**. Self assessment is performed by the internal auditors supplemented by an external review conducted by a consulting firm.

The Banking Advisory Group favours the approach of self assessment with independent review, for the following reasons:
- It allows capitalisation of the organisation's internal auditor skills, of their experience in the completion of audit assignments, and of their knowledge of internal and external guidelines.
- It engages internal auditors in areas other than their own, in a spirit of respect for the criteria of independence, so enabling auditors to learn from the operation of another internal audit entity.
- Its costs are definitely lower, since the work is mostly performed in–house.
- It is a truly participative Project.

The scope of QAR includes the review of:
- The expectations of the activity as expressed by its "clients"
- The control environment in the entity and the audit practice environment of the Chief Audit Executive
- The method of evaluation of enterprise risk, by assessing organisational controls, and including aspects of the governance process in audit plans to ensure that audit activities add value to the enterprise
- The integration of internal auditing into the organisation's governance process, including the attendant relationships and communications between and among the key groups involved in that process, so aligning audit objectives and plans with the strategic objectives of the entity as a whole
- Compliance to Standards
- The mix of knowledge, experience, and disciplines within the staff, including staff focus on process improvement and value-added activities
- The tools and techniques employed by the department, with emphasis on the use of technology

For more details, please refer to Appendix 4.

Banking Advisory Group Position on the Organisation and Components of Banking Internal Control

Even though the different lines of defence described in this chapter can be applied in various ways within the Organisation, the bottom line remains the same: everyone is involved in the internal control system and should have a specific role to play.

Support for a control culture from the Executive management and the Board, as well as the involvement of all staff members, are essential contributory factors. All those involved need to know their role and feel responsible for the achievement of their control objectives.

The assessment of each level of control at the level immediately above makes the system dynamic and continuously progressive. Internal audit monitors the effectiveness of the internal control framework in use by operational staff and specialised functions (Risk Management, Compliance). Internal audit issues recommendations when improvements need to be made.

Internal Audit should also ensure that the organisation of Permanent Control is consistent and runs efficiently, and that there are neither loopholes nor overlap between the internal control functions.

The audit function is, in turn, assessed at the very least by
– regulators to make sure that all regulatory requirements are met,
– Quality Assurance Reviews that check that all the professional standards are met and ensure that the governance of the function is compliant with the requirements of independence.

Moreover, in some countries such as Luxembourg, internal audit is also assessed by external auditors.

Internal auditors are therefore subject to the same obligations as their auditees. We feel that this framework shows our clients that we apply to ourselves what we ask of them and consequently enhances the credibility of the function.

41

Part 3

Banking Internal Auditing

Part 3 Banking Internal Auditing

3.1.   Internal Auditing Reporting Lines – The Question of Independence

Standard 1100 states that *"the internal audit activity should be independent, and internal auditors should be objective in performing their work"*. This Standard adds that: *"the Chief Audit Executive should report to a level within the organization that allows the internal audit activity to fulfil its responsibilities"*.

The principle of independence is a prerequisite mentioned by the BAG Survey respondents.
For example, the Slovenian Banking Act states that: *"the bank shall organise its internal audit as an independent unit which is directly subordinated to the bank's management board and is separate from other organisational units"*.

This independence requirement must be articulated in the Organisation. It should obey strict governance rules. As shown in section 2.2.3., depending on the corporate governance bodies of the Organisation and on national regulations (whether prescriptive or not), two types of reporting line are in evidence:
–   Direct reporting line to Executive management
–   Direct reporting line to the Board (directly or via an Audit Committee)
In cases where the internal audit function reports to Executive management, it is appropriate, as recommended by the Basel Committee document *"Enhancing Corporate Governance for Banking Organisations"* (February 2006), to have a second reporting line (dotted line type) to a supervisory body (Board of Directors, Supervisory Board, Board, Collegio Sindacale[11], Audit Committee, etc.).

---

[11]   The Collegio Sindacale is part of the corporate governance model in Italian civil law and is tasked with control and supervisory missions. The Collegio Sindacale is responsible for overseeing the Internal Control System. As part of this, the Collegio Sindacale is involved in the recruitment of the Chief Audit Executive. It periodically receives the results of Internal Audit assessments and can meet the Chief Audit Executive privately without Executive management being present.

This reporting line can materialise close relationships with this governance body, notably direct access without the imposed approval of Executive management. In relation to Audit Committees, several European countries have no regulation. It may explain why only two out of three of the CBOK respondent banks have an Audit Committee. However, the Audit Committee is recognised as best practice.

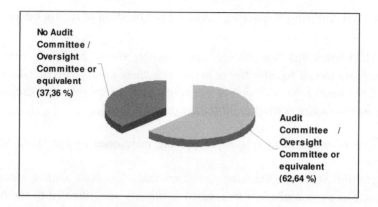

No Audit Committee / Oversight Committee or equivalent (37,36 %)

Audit Committee / Oversight Committee or equivalent (62,64 %)

Figure 3: Percentage of organizations having an Audit Committee (Source: CBOK survey 2006).

The responsibilities usually assigned to Audit Committees in regard to the internal audit function are the following:
– oversight of the internal auditing of the bank
– review and approval of the scope of audit scope and of the multi-annual audit plan
– definition and approval of resources (budget, financial resources…)
– review of the completion of the audit plan
– receipt of audit reports, including the assurance that management is taking appropriate corrective action in a timely manner to address control weaknesses, non-compliance with policies, laws and regulations, and other problems identified by auditors
– discuss of matters with the Chief Audit Executive (CAE) without the presence of the Executive management

The Audit Committee also examines:
– the relations and contacts with regulatory authorities
– the annual report on internal control

As the European 8th Directive adopted in 2008 makes the existence of an Audit Committee mandatory for listed companies and public interest entities (including banks), there will be reinforcement of the Audit Committee's link to internal auditing; and of the independence of the entire Function.

Our position is that the Audit Committee is an essential body of Corporate Governance. The CAE should be able to meet the Chair of the Audit Committee independently, i.e. without the presence of the Executive management.

3.2. Appointment and Evaluation of the Chief Audit Executive (CAE)

The graph below (Figure 4) shows that 40% of CAEs are appointed by the chairperson of the Board or the Audit Committee. This implies that 60% are still not appointed by an independent body.

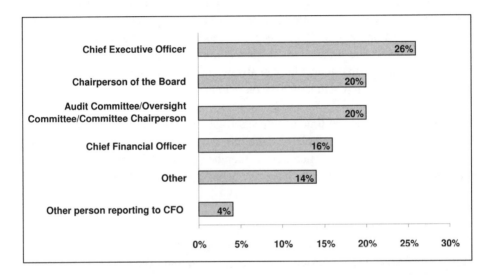

Figure 4: Persons involved in appointing the CAE (source: CBOK survey 2006).

One of the reasons for this state of affairs is that European regulation does not specify clearly by whom the CAE should be appointed.

We believe that evaluation of the CAE should be performed by the body or person to whom the CAE reports. Should this be Executive management, we consider it to be good practice that the Board or its Audit Committee should be involved.

In addition, the CAE should also be evaluated in part by the review of the function itself, in the course of Quality Assurance Reviews (see section 2.2.5.2. on the assessment of the Periodic Control) or by means of feedback from auditees.

We believe auditees' opinions to be a necessary part of the process. However, to maintain the full independence of the internal auditing function, we consider that it should not be linked to an audit assignment. Hence the gathering of auditee opinion should be done either annually or during a quality assurance review.

3.3.   Information Communicated to Internal Auditing

Full access by Internal Audit to information is normally required by the IIA Standards and local regulation (see Practice Advisory 1130–1).

In addition, we believe that the CAE, at least, should be actively informed of all major issues or events that could have an impact on the present or future activities of the Organisation, so that, if necessary, the audit plan can be updated or special assignments scheduled. Indeed, to adequately and efficiently assess the risks to the Bank, it is necessary that the audit plan always matches the objectives and activities of the Organisation (IIA standard 2010 on planning).

In order to be informed in time of any significant changes in the Organisation, the CAE should at least be a recipient of the minutes of the various bank management meetings. Although not a permanent member, the CAE should attend these meetings as an observer any time he or she believes it to be necessary.

3.4.   Organisation of Internal Auditing

Most of the time, the organisation of banking Internal Audit reflects the bank's organisation and is thus structured by business line and geographical zone.
"Internal Audit Division is organised in eight Departments: Retail, Corporate Banking, Private Banking and Asset Management, Financial Markets, Operations, Accounting, IT and Employees. This organisation reflects, with necessary adjustments, the model of organisational management and executive coordination in the Bank." (Portuguese BAG Survey respondent)
Naturally, the internal audit department of a small entity is not organised in the same way as a big company or a multinational firm. However as banking organisations have to face increasingly specific risks, internal auditing needs more expertise and therefore must set up departments dedicated to auditing these risks.

Below, we describe the major internal audit structures. This is in order to identify the criteria which should be taken into consideration when choosing a model to enhance the efficiency of the internal audit organisation.

3.4.1. Description of the Major Models in Internal Auditing

The different internal audit structures can be summarised in the following models:
- centralised using specialised teams or a pool of multi-disciplinary auditors
- decentralised
- mixed (centralised – decentralised)

3.4.1.1. Centralised Internal Auditing

The centralised structure implies that generally both the means and the management team are based in a single location.
Two types of centralised organisations exist, the specialised (Figure 5) and the multi-disciplinary structures (Figure 6, page 50).

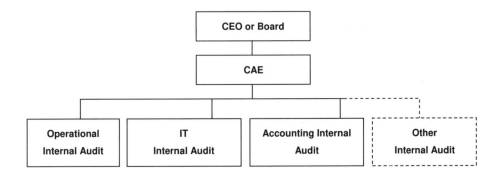

Figure 5: Specialised structure model.

The specialised structure is divided into specific audit teams. The auditors of each team have similar skills and therefore undertake activities in the same specific domain. This structure facilitates the integration of specialists within the internal audit department, and allows the scope of internal auditing to extend to all the activities of the Bank. In addition, it facilitates the dialogue between the operational staff and the auditor, because all have the same culture and speak the same language. It should be borne in mind that specialised internal audit teams require exchanges of skills and/or competencies between and among the teams; hence the need for a more complex method of staff management and work planning. In the long run, in order to maintain the independence of the auditors, turnover between the teams and cross-utilisation of staff between different specialisations, should be promoted as far as possible.

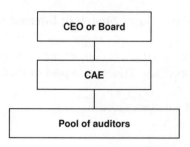

Figure 6: Multi-disciplinary structure model.

In the multi-disciplinary structure, senior and junior auditors are gathered in a pool. For each mission, teams are set up according to the availability and capability of each auditor. This structure develops auditors by providing more diversified experience, which can be more motivating for the individual. This structure makes the management of the internal audit department staff easier. However, to maintain work of high quality, Internal Audit may have to use outside service providers when it manages missions requiring specific competencies not found internally.

3.4.1.2. Decentralised Internal Auditing

A decentralised structure allows for more integration into the organisation and thus for a better understanding of the operational activities. In international groups, the decentralised organisation is the natural model, due to the logistical and cost issues.

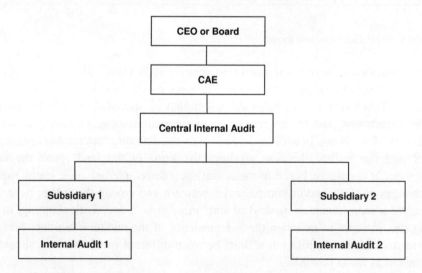

Figure 7: Decentralised structure model.

The decentralised structure implies the existence of a central internal audit department, which provides certain services (Standards / Reference department, Training department, tools, etc.). However, because of the decentralisation, the central internal audit department may have less understanding of and control over the activities of the subsidiaries, which implies that it is more difficult to monitor risks. In the case of very small audit entities (there could be a single auditor), it is more difficult to develop local expertise.

3.4.1.3. Mixed Structure

The mixed structure (Figure 8) combines a centralised structure (specialised teams and/or pool of multi-disciplinary auditors) and a decentralised structure (audit in subsidiaries). The advantages of the mixed structure are those of the decentralised approach, namely the greater understanding of the Organisation, and more flexibility when undertaking the work.

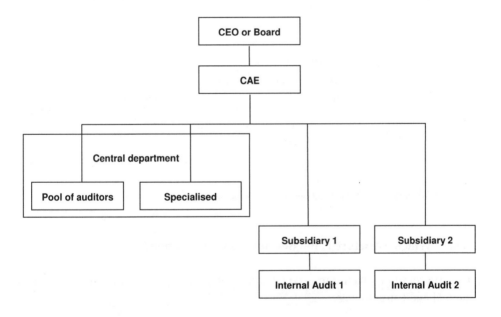

Figure 8: Mixed Structure model.

In economic terms mixed organisation also permits the mutualisation of skills and allows the "small internal audit entities" to benefit from the skills and competencies of the highly specialised auditors of the centralised function.

We wish to highlight that the success of this model relies upon
- the oversight by the central internal audit department of the work in the subsidiaries and
- the clear division of responsibilities between the central internal audit department and the local audits.

3.4.1.4. Advantages and Disadvantages of Each Structure

	Advantages	Disadvantages
Specialised Structure	– Competencies – Credibility	More complex staff management and work planning
Multi-disciplinary structure	– Facilitate management of staff – Diversity of experiences enhancing motivation	Less skilled in specific and complex matters
Centralised structure	– Independence – Uniqueness – Circulation of information	Further removed from operational expectations at the subsidiary level
Decentralised structure	– Understanding of local cultures – Flexibility	Difficulty of monitoring the subsidiaries
Mix of centralised and decentralised structure	Advantages of the centralised and the decentralised structure	Onerousness

Table 2: Advantages and disadvantages of each structure.

3.4.2. Which Structure is the Best for the Organisation?

The criteria to be taken into account when determining the best and most efficient internal audit structure are:

- **Structure of the Organisation audited**
  Is the Bank organised by geographical area, into activity sectors or a mixture of both? The mapping of the auditable areas will depend on the answer.

- **Level of complexity of banking activities**
  Does the audit team have the appropriately skilled staff to cover the Bank's activities efficiently?

The mechanisms to be used to provide sufficient skills are:
− training existing auditors
− outsourcing assignments to specialists
− using skilled staff from other entities in the group
  See section 3.4.3. "Is the outsourcing of internal auditing a contradiction in terms?" for more details.

• **Optimisation of management of resources**
  The size of the Organisation or of the sub-organisation audited will be a determining factor in making the choice of specialised or general teams. Further, as described above, specialised teams ensure a better quality audit but are less flexible in management terms .

• **Adequate and efficient reporting of information to the CAE**
  The CAE must be informed of the internal control level in all the subsidiaries. Hence the need to ensure the consistency of the audit methodology, of the internal references and audit tools and of reporting.
  See section 3.4.4. "Multinational operations" for more details.

> In conclusion, the internal audit structure may be a combination of different models. But it must above all retain the capacity to adapt to environmental changes. In order to bridge gaps in expertise, we believe that one of the best solutions for a large business organisation is to uphold a mix of specialised teams alongside a "common pool" of multi-disciplinary auditors (which does not preclude the latter also having specialist interests such as IT, accounting, trading, etc.).

3.4.3. Is the Outsourcing of Internal Audit a contradiction in terms?

It may appear contradictory to outsource internal auditing. Outsourcing however can be acceptable to the regulator under specific conditions:
1. group audit to perform audit assignments in the subsidiaries, which is a form of "internal outsourcing", i.e. within the scope of the Group
2. provided the audit does not concern the core activities of the banking organisation
3. provided the audit team has insufficient skills to perform the assignment (i.e.: BASEL II pre-validation, Mathematical Models,…)

Figure 9 (page 54) shows that about 80% of banking organisations outsource or co-source between 10% and 20% of their internal audit activity (CBOK survey).

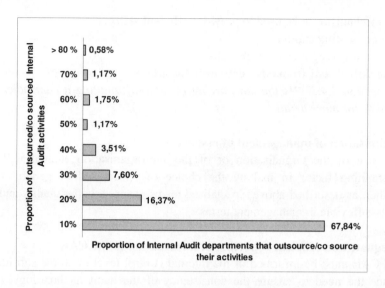

Figure 9: Percentage internal audit activities currently outsourced/co sourced (Source: CBOK survey 2006).

The graph below (Figure 10) completes the picture by showing the change in the outsourced/co-sourced activities budget. For 52% of internal audit departments, the budget remains the same, but for about 40% it will increase. The second scenario could be explained by the increasing need for specialist expertise and skills in the internal audit department, a need which could be met by outsourcing.

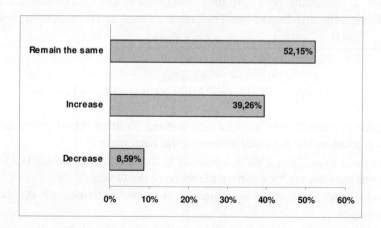

Figure 10: Change in outsourced / co sourced activities budget (Source: CBOK survey 2006).

There are different types of outsourcing / co-sourcing:
- outsourcing the whole assignment to specialists external to the Organisation
- integrate an external specialist to an internally managed mission
- perform audits jointly with specialists from the Head Office

---

Our position is that it will almost invariably be a better solution to outsource internal auditing, rather than audit without the necessary skills, or not to undertake the audit at all, in order to avoid outsourcing.

In every case, especially including outsourced internal auditing, the procedures must remain under the supervision and the responsibility of the entity which has delegated the task. This means that:
- The contract with the outsource provider must clearly state that internal auditing will retain responsibility for the work and is entitled to challenge the work both in progress and on completion.
- Even if the internal audit department does not have specialist teams, the CAE should ensure that s/he has auditors providing an assurance that the issue has been handled with due diligence.

3.4.4. Multinational Operations

In the case of international banking groups, two complementary rules should be applied and taken into account when considering the efficiency of the internal audit function.

The first rule is to follow the regulation on the internal control of the parent company in the relevant national market. An exception arises when the regulation of the country of the subsidiary is stricter than the home regulation of the parent company.

"Local branches and subsidiaries must also abide by the rules and regulations set by their local regulator." (Swedish BAG Survey respondent)

The second rule is to adhere to the regulatory requirement of the country of location. To comply with this rule, it will be more efficient to have a decentralised audit team in each subsidiary. If the audit were totally centralised, the auditors in the Head office would have to be acquainted in detail with all the regulations of all the countries concerned.

In both these cases, efficiency requires that the internal control procedures of multinational banking organisations ensure that the management and execution of operations and the behaviour of employees abide by the guidelines of the Bank's activities stated by its corporate governance bodies, as well as by applicable laws and regulations and by the internal principles, standards and rules of the Organisation.

That is surely the reason why the Belgian and the German respondents cited the need for an additional line of defence for the multinational banking organisations, in the form of the Group Audit. The objectives of Group Audit are to monitor and ensure that audit Standards are consistently applied throughout the whole group. In some entities, the function of Group Audit is performed by the Inspection Générale (as is the case in France).

Banking Advisory Group Position on the Organisation and Positioning of Banking Internal Auditing

In order to ensure its efficiency and achieve its objectives, Banking Internal Audit should comply with several prerequisites:

1. Ensure the independence of the Chief Audit Executive:
– Position of the CAE at the top level of the organisation with direct reporting to the Board of Directors or, if reporting to the Executive Management, a second reporting line (dotted line) to a supervisory body (Board of Directors, Audit Committee, etc). It appears more and more necessary to reinforce the link with the Board of Directors or the Chairman of the Audit Committee. In particular, the CAE must have a direct access to them at any time, in addition to the scheduled regular meetings. Over and above these reporting considerations, it is important that governance bodies be aware of the internal control culture.
– Appointment and evaluation of the CAE should be shared between Management and the chairperson of the Audit Committee. Best practice is that the Audit Committee is routinely involved in the appointment and discharge of the CAE and that this involvement is stated in the Audit Committee charter.

2. Ensure that the CAE has full access to all the information needed for the achievement of his/her objectives.

3. Ensure that the Internal Audit structure is the most efficient for the organisation, taking into account the structure of the organisation itself, the complexity of the activities under review, the resources themselves and the mechanisms for reporting to the CAE.

4. Ensure an adequate level of expertise for all audit assignments
The internal audit department should possess all the expertise required to cover the activities performed within the Bank. However, in an environment where activities are increasingly complex, internal audit can ask for assistance from external providers. These external resources should remain under the supervision of the head of the internal audit department.

3.5. Role and Scope of Banking Internal Auditing

The IIA Standard 1000 requirements state that the proper scope and role of each internal audit department must be set out in an internal audit charter approved by the Board of the bank.

The internal audit charter is a formal written document which:
–   Establishes the position of the internal audit activity position within the organisation
–   Authorises access to records, personnel, and physical properties relevant to the performance of engagements, and
–   Defines the scope of internal audit activities.

The Basel Committee also states that: *"each bank should have an internal audit charter that enhances the standing and authority of the internal audit function within the bank"* (Internal Audit in Banks and supervisor's relationships with auditors: 6th principle, see Appendix 6).

3.5.1. Role of Banking Internal Auditing

The IIA defines the role of internal auditing in Standard 2100 – Nature of Work – as follows: *"the internal audit activity should evaluate and contribute to the improvement of risk management, control, and governance processes using a systematic and disciplined approach"*.

The BAG Survey respondent from Luxembourg added more details to this definition.
"The internal audit department should determine whether:
–   *the system for the identification, measurement and control of risks is operating satisfactorily*
–   *securities and other assets are being properly administered*
–   *transactions are being correctly executed*
–   *transactions are being completely and accurately recorded and reliably and promptly reported*
–   *company operations and organisation comply with relevant rules and regulations*
–   *decisions made by Management and by those duly authorised by it are put into action and established procedures for the conduct of banking business or applicable to the credit institution, are complied with."*

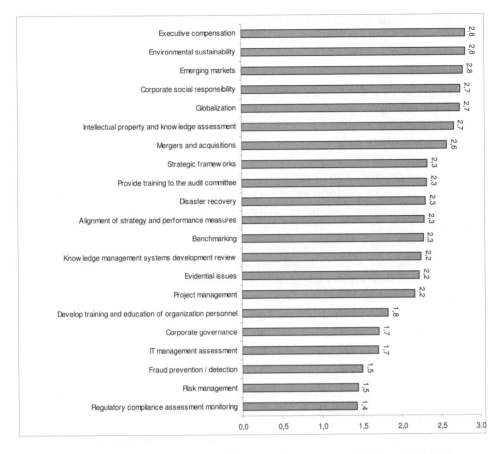

Figure 11: Role (defined as being within the scope of internal audit) that the internal audit function currently has in its organization or will have in the next 3 years. (1: currently has role; 2: likely to have a role within the next 3 years; 3: unlikely to have a role). (Source: CBOK survey 2006).

The graph in Figure 11 indicates that the activities most frequently audited today by banking internal auditors are:
– regulatory compliance assessment monitoring
– risk management
– fraud prevention / Detection
– IT management assessment
– corporate governance
– developing training and education on the internal control of organisation personnel

59

This graph also shows that the focus of banking internal auditing in the next 3 years will be on the following areas:
– project management
– evidential issues
– knowledge management systems development review
– benchmarking
– alignment of strategy and performance measures
– disaster recovery

According to the BAG Survey, internal audit departments within European banking organisations **mainly perform assurance** rather than **consulting assignments**. Assurance assignments consist of analysing the management of operational and compliance engagements.

The role of internal auditing is not only to check and verify the compliance with procedures and their correct application. IA is evolving more towards evaluation of the adequacy of what is in place. That means that IA is responsible for assessing the effectiveness of the internal control framework and risk management within the Organisation. This is enforced by the new Basel Capital Accord (Basel II) particularly Pillar II on the supervisory review and evaluation processes.

Is Internal Auditing an *ex post* control function?

Whereas permanent control has the function – non exclusive – of an *ex ante* control, with risk monitoring being in real time, the role of internal auditing is stated to be ex post. Thus internal auditing takes place after events have occurred, i.e. fraud, operational deficiencies, counterparty default, etc.

The BAG considers that this vision is simplistic.

Internal auditing does not simply mean "looking at the driving mirror".

Internal auditing has a privileged position in the Organisation, ensures global and updated risk assessment. The indicators at its disposal are warning signs enabling internal auditing to play a preventive role.

It is important, in our view and at this time, that internal auditing be provided with the tools and resources allowing it to disclose and to anticipate important deficiencies.

Although the audit of financial engagements may be necessary, some auditors, like the Bulgarian BAG Survey respondent, perceive this task as a "*duplication of the external auditors' work*". Regulatory audits (MIFID, Basel II, Business Continuity Plan, etc.) are also becoming more frequent, since their performance is mandatory under certain national regulations. Hence, in addition to the checks performed on procedures and their application, the role of internal auditing is moving towards a more complete analysis of the adequacy of specific frameworks.

As we know, fraud occurs in the banking sector, as in every sector or industry. Indeed, there is no system of control able to provide more than a "reasonable assurance" that the risk of fraud is properly identified and evaluated, and that there is an adequate framework to prevent it.

Given that it is unable to eradicate fraudulent activity (or behaviour), the contribution of internal auditing to fraud prevention may be summarised as:
–   assessing the framework and the efficiency of the controls over the risk of fraud
–   detecting and investigating fraud cases
–   issuing recommendations for upgrading the various lines of defence
–   reporting matters to Executive Management and to the Board

In addition, despite the content of Standards 1210.A2, and notably in fraud cases, the duties of internal auditing could extend to the identification of individual responsibilities. Sanctions, if any, should be handed out by Management, since Audit is not an operational function.

If the primary role of internal auditing is security, it has a more pressing duty to provide advice to the Organisation. As a consequence, in addition to its assurance activities, Internal Audit could be involved in working groups, as local regulators increasingly require Internal Audit to participate in key projects (notably in Germany).
However, there is a line not to be crossed. Internal Audit should not play a leading role in these working groups. To do so would give rise to a conflict of interest and would compromise independence.
The role of Internal Audit in consulting activity should be limited to providing advice on best practices (in the internal control and risk management fields).

The Banking Advisory Group considers that internal audit resources / skills should be placed at the disposal of Executive management, for use if needed.
Should any consulting assignment be involved, this should not be under the leadership of Internal Audit.

A "grey zone" may exist in the audit of the "pre-implementation review" performed at each step of the delivery of a big project. In this case, audit has to avoid becoming involved in operational responsibilities. This is because it would be difficult for Internal Audit to perform subsequent auditing missions, after having more or less validated a project.

3.5.2. Scope of Banking Internal Auditing

According to all the respondents of the BAG Survey respondents, Internal Audit may intervene in any domain of the bank:

- *"Internal audit has to audit all existing procedures within the banks."* (Turkish BAG Survey respondent)
- *"Internal audit has a universe which covers all products, process and systems."* (British BAG Survey respondent)

Internal auditors should have access to all documents, to all properties and to all people within the organisation. This principle must apply to every entity in the group.

"The scope of the internal audit department [...] should be extended to the foreign branches and to subsidiaries both in the home country and abroad. The internal audit department should make regular site visits to branches." (Luxembourg BAG Survey respondent)

3.5.2.1. Auditing Corporate Governance

Limits to the scope of Internal Audit may exist with regard to corporate governance audits dealing with the relations between Executive management and the Board at the parent company level. Since Internal Audit is one of the players in the Governance field and reports either to the Executive management and/or the Board, it is not in a position to assess these Governance Bodies. Attempts at auditing its own management are likely to put Internal Audit into a difficult situation and could lead to its independence and its objectivity being impaired or curtailed . Nevertheless, as the Governance Bodies do need to be evaluated, the Banking Advisory Group considers that this should be performed by an external body. Even so, Internal Audit can and should place at the disposal of the Governance bodies, its knowledge, its tools, and its expertise, so assisting the Board. In this situation, Internal Audit plays the role of consultant.

With regard to Corporate Governance within the subsidiaries, and to the risk management and control processes at that level, Internal Audit should assess and contribute to their improvement. But when seeking to improve Governance, internal audit assignments should not be conducted by auditors belonging to the subsidiary. The audits should be performed by auditors belonging to the Group (central level).

With reference to the Basel Committee document of February 2006 on Corporate Governance, the key points to be assessed are:

- Is there an Audit Committee or an equivalent structure within the subsidiary?
- What is its composition? Does it have the required skills and competencies?
- Do the auditors have easy and regular access to the Audit Committee?
- Are the flows of information (bottom-up, top down) sufficient to allow efficient decision-making and management?
- Does Executive management have an appropriate oversight over the Internal Control system?
- Does the Board of Directors periodically assess the effectiveness of its own governance practices?
- Are Corporate values and Codes of conduct duly defined by the Corporate Governance Bodies?

The other aspects of Governance, especially operational Governance, undoubtedly fall within the scope of Internal Audit. In this case, Operational Governance is defined as the means of implementing Corporate Governance principles and decisions throughout all the entities of the group.

In order to assess operational Governance, Internal Audit should notably review:
- governance structures in the entities
- compliance to ethical values
- the independence of the internal audit function when the review is performed by the central and not local audit team
- etc.

3.5.2.2. Audit Plan

To cover the full scope of the organisation within a reasonable time frame, the internal audit function needs a comprehensive multi-annual audit plan which should be updated each year. Standard 2010 – Planning states that:

"The chief audit executive should establish risk-based plans to determine the priorities of the internal audit activity, consistent with the organization's goals".

"The basis for the development of the annual audit plan is risk assessment, which should determine significant areas and processes to be subjected to review. Risk assessment identifies and considers either internal risks and issues (such as change in the organizational structure, new products, new objectives and projects for the bank, rotation of personnel and managers, new IT applications and systems), or external risks and issues (changes in economic environment, changes in competitor

activities, technological progress, new laws and regulations) which can adversely affect the achievement of the objectives set. Management should be involved in the process of Annual Audit Planning (AAP) to ensure that the AAP is coherent with the bank's objectives." (Polish BAG Survey respondent)

Figure 12 on page 65 confirms the view from the Polish BAG Survey respondent. One out of five CBOK respondents uses a risk-based methodology to establish the audit plan. That "only" 20% use a risk-based methodology is surprising, as this method is the most objective and thorough. It relies on risk ratings obtained from a documented methodology (questionnaires, interviews etc) applied to the identified auditable domains.

Risk and Control Approach: the Swing of the Pendulum

As a result of the control approach being considered too formal and routine, thereby avoiding the real issues, the risk approach was adopted. In the wake of the current market crisis, and especially the "bankruptcy" of Northern Rock, the question arises (and has been posed by the FSA) as to whether in a market that is in turmoil and fast changing, the control approach should be reassessed.

The Banking Advisory Group considers that the risk mapping carried out by Internal Audit has only a qualified vision. It is no more than snapshot of the risks at any one time. The history of incidents shows that they may occur where they are not expected, and for unexpected amounts. Although it is true that audit work must be focused on the main identified risk areas, it is also true that IA should assess the internal control system within identified low risk areas. This is the meaning of the term "completeness" of the audit plan, in a reasonable periodic cycle.

The second source of the audit plan is compliance/regulatory requirements (15% of citings). As we saw in section 3.5.1 on the Role of Banking Internal Auditing; regulators expect to obtain more and more value from the internal audit departments. Indeed, there are even more stringent requirements laid upon them, that they review, on an annual basis, specific subjects (anti-money laundering, Basel II, MiFID, etc.).

Requests from management are cited as the source of the audit plan in 14% of cases. This is not surprising, since management is one of the clients of internal audit. The fact that the number is so high, could also be interpreted as meaning that Internal Audit is not yet independent enough to identify its assignments itself. We consider that the internal audit department should listen to management's suggestions, but decide independently which assignments it will perform.

Consultation of the previous years audit plan as being an element establishing the audit plan came in fourth position with almost 14%. This answer is understandable since internal auditing should design a multi-annual plan in order to make sure that all auditable domains are reviewed in a reasonable timeframe. Definition of priorities over a 3 year period, with reassessment each year to verify if they are still applicable, is a strategy that helps put the risks of the whole company into perspective and avoids focussing too narrowly on the current risk situation.

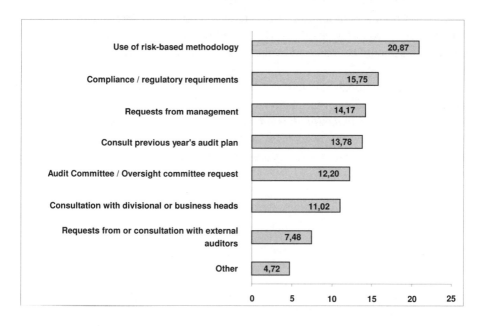

Figure 12: Definition of the audit plan (Source: CBOK survey 2006).

3.5.3. Cooperation with External Auditors

External auditing and internal auditing are complementary. The IIA Standard 2020 – Coordination – states that: "*the chief audit executive should share information and coordinate activities with other internal and external providers of relevant assurance and consulting services to ensure proper coverage and minimize duplication of effort*". The synergy between internal auditing and external auditing helps improve the internal control system of the bank. However, the level of synergy and cooperation vary greatly from one country to another, mostly because of cultural practices and the history of working with an external audit firm. Trust and confidence between internal and external audit should undoubtedly be established, because it will lead to greater cooperation.

65

Once such trust is established, internal and external auditors should communicate frequently in order to avoid redundancy or duplication in the conduct of assignments. This communication also helps in sharing views on the risk management and internal control frameworks of the organisation. Internal Audit should be informed of the potential shortfalls identified by external auditors in order to understand the risks and take action as required. Whereas external auditors issue recommendations, it is considered best practice for Internal Audit to be involved in the follow-up of their implementation.

The plans of both sets of auditors are usually coordinated to spread audit coverage. Outputs are frequently exchanged in order to improve efficiency. These arrangements should be managed by the Audit Committee, when it exists.

The future International Standard on Auditing, ISA 610, will strengthen the link between internal and external auditors. The stated Objective in §6 is for external audit *"to obtain an understanding of the internal audit function and determine whether the activities of the internal audit function are relevant to planning and performing the audit and, if relevant, the effect on the procedures performed by the external auditor."*

Banking Advisory Group Position on the Scope and the Role of Banking Internal Auditing

With internal auditing in recent years becoming a more professional function, it seems undeniable that its role is to assist an organisation better evaluate and contribute to the improvement of the processes of risk management, control and governance. But how internal audit does so is the most interesting question. Performing assurance and consulting engagements is not enough. The questions of where and how need to be addressed.

Where?

The scope of internal audit should be the entire organisation; as its scope should not in any way be limited. If competencies are missing in regard to a specific and technical matter, the CAE should either recruit an auditor with the necessary skills, or outsource the assignment while retaining oversight.

How?

The audit plan should be defined on a pluri-annual basis, where an assessment is made each year. This will allow for better prioritisation and ensure coverage of the full scope. A risk-based methodology to design the audit plan is of the utmost importance, as this is the only means available to a factual, objective and documented approach to identify and rate risks. Even though there is no perfect risk assessment method, there is no reason not to perform one! Believing that it is good practice that all the internal control actors use the same mapping of "auditable domains" as a common basis of discussion, we are also of the view that they should have their own risk assessment, as they will be analysing different factors depending on their specific targets. Coordinating and exchanging the results of these risk assessments should be favoured.

Finally, keeping a close communication relationship with management and regulators will also help target their requirements and consequently integrate the necessary assignments into the audit plan.

With regards to the new Basel II Regulation, the internal audit work load has increased. The number of auditors in the Internal Audit Department should be correlated to the scope of the work undertaken. Numbers should not be a fixed percentage of employees in the organization, as usually the case.

3.6.   Profile and Career Path of Auditors

3.6.1. Specific Skills and Competencies Required from a Banking Internal Auditor

The Basel Committee (8th principle, see Appendix 6) as well as IIA Standard 1210 require that not only internal auditors but also the internal audit function as a whole possess a high level of multidisciplinary competencies. In order to be able to address all the risks of the organisation and to conduct assignments in an effective manner, chief audit executives have to recruit auditors with the necessary skills and competencies.

What are these skills? What mix of competencies and experience level does an auditor need? Will these skills evolve in the coming years?

Under recruitment guidelines, the specific skills of an internal auditor are:
– *"ability to work independently*
– *ability to work effectively under pressure and to tight deadlines*
– *good project management and problem solving skills*
– *accurate and quality focused mindset*
– *good presentation and communication skills*
– *high integrity and discretion."* (German BAG Survey respondent)

– *"Awareness of the IIA Professional Practices Framework, of the concepts of the COSO framework and international best practice*
– *team player with an open mindset working as an integral part of an audit team*
– *excellent communication and interpersonal skills*
– *commitment to personal development*
– *analytical skills*
– *accounting or banking background is an advantage."* (The Swedish BAG Survey respondent)

There is no "unique auditor profile." However, it seems that banking auditors should possess competencies which fall into two areas: "Technical knowledge" and "Behavioural skills". They should also possess a certain level of education and professional background.

3.6.1.1. Technical Knowledge

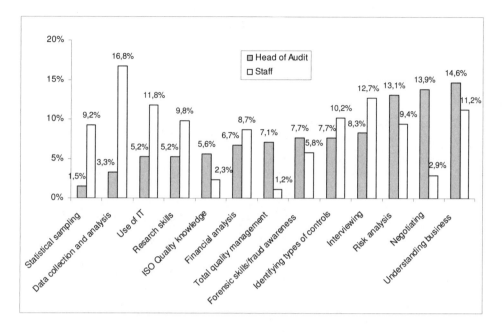

Figure 13: Technical skills required at different levels of responsibility (Source: CBOK survey 2006).

From a technical perspective, as shown in the graph above, the main specific technical skills to be possessed by a European banking internal audit team are the following:
– data collection and analysis (16.8% for staff and 3.3% for head of audit)
– understanding business (14.6% for head of audit and 11.2% for staff)
– negotiating (13.9% for head of audit and 2.9% for staff)
– risk analysis (13.1% for head of audit and 9.4% for staff)
– interviewing (12.7 % for the staff and 8.3% for head of audit)
– use of IT (11.8% for staff and 5.2% for head of audit)

These skills are a prerequisite for teams to be able to identify and address the risks of the Organisation, to evaluate the internal controls and the corporate governance processes. It must be emphasised how complex are the various banking activities. These activities require more and more expertise in various areas. Consequently, understanding the technical business processes is essential for internal auditors, as it allows them to perform in-depth and accurate investigations and to issue operational and value-added recommendations.
This is particularly the case in those banks where multi businesses and complex activities exist.

69

Even though not a technical skill recognised as formally necessary by chief audit executives, we consider that internal auditors should also be able to the identify indicators that can help prevent and detect fraud.

3.6.1.2. Behavioural Skills

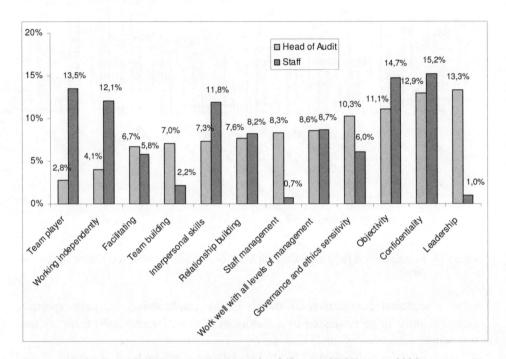

Figure 14: Behavioural skills for each professional level (Source: CBOK survey 2006).

When recruiting internal auditors, chief audit executives should also consider non-technical skills. This is because internal auditors are often considered as "high potentials" or "high fliers" within the banks. As shown by the graph above, valued behavioural skills are:
– Confidentiality (15.2%)
– Objectivity (14.7%)
– Team player (13.5%)
– Working independently (12.1%)
– Interpersonal skills (11.8%)
Beyond these skills, internal auditors should be able to communicate and discuss their audit conclusions and findings with auditees at the right level, that is, at the appropriate level, from operational staff to top management. This implies the need for considerable adaptability, sound judgement, the ability to convince and; in some instances, the necessary courage.

In addition to the skills and competencies already highlighted, internal auditors should also be able to:
- follow the evolution of risks, because the financial market is continuously evolving
- understand the IT environment, because it is changing rapidly
- use IT tools to gather and analyse the data whose volume is continuously increasing

The chief audit executive should also ensure that the audit team presents enough cultural diversity to address the changing needs of an increasingly global market.
Indeed, an audit team which mixes staff from different cultures and geographic backgrounds is better able to address various situations and expand the internal control culture within the organisation.

3.6.1.3. Education, Background and Certification

"Apart from the necessary technical skills inherent to the audit function, auditors must also have a reasonable background in terms of other areas of knowledge, either specific (accounting, management, information systems, etc.) or specifically banking-related." (Portuguese BAG Survey respondent)
Ideally, banking chief audit executives need people with a high level of formal education (49% of internal auditors have a master degree level, see Figure 15 on page 72), completed by some initial professional experience.

Accounting/Finance, IT and Market Model skills are considered increasingly important in the banking sector as:
- the business lines are more and more technical, requiring continuously higher expertise
- the financial products are more and more complex
- the level of straight-through processing system is growing
- the compliance to Basel II requirements calls for Risk Model development

This has resulted in an increasing importance given to Accounting/Finance/ Mathematical Models and IT systems.

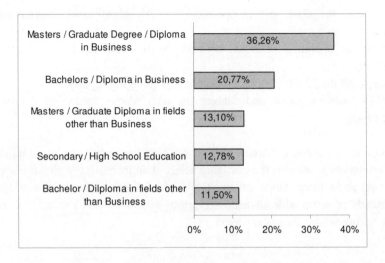

Figure 15: Highest level of formal education for internal auditors (excluding certification)
(Source: CBOK survey 2006).

Certifications are also appreciated and increasingly required.

For a great majority of European banks, the CIA (Certified Internal Auditor) or the UK and Ireland equivalent, the MIIA, is highly recommended. It is also compulsory in one Swiss organisation.

Other certifications may be requested, for auditors who are specialised in a specific activity:

- CISA (Certified Information Systems Auditor)
- CPA (Certified Public Accountants)
- CFSA (Certified Financial Services Auditor)

As the financial markets and the banking environment are continuously evolving, the recruitment of staff with sufficient skills and competencies is not enough. The chief audit executive should oversee the continuing adequacy of the internal auditors' competencies and expertise, and the improvement of the knowledge levels of the audit team.

Improvement can be attained by:

- planning training activities appropriate to each auditor's duties
- rotating the auditors' duties
- participating in seminars organised by the bank or by the local Institute of Internal Auditors or the local banking federation
- participating in foreign seminars with other banks
- sharing best practice with other banks (benchmarking)

The Chief Audit Executive must also effectively manage the turnover in the audit teams in order to preserve levels of knowledge within the function.

3.6.2. Attractiveness of Internal Audit Function and Career Path

"A career as an internal auditor is today attractive. It is therefore relatively easy to hire qualified people, from junior to senior profiles." (Finnish BAG Survey respondent)

.*"Internal auditor positions are very attractive. However, the market is not reflecting this trend, as newcomers are seeking for employment in departments that generate profits."* (Swiss BAG Survey respondent)

"There is a clear career path out of internal audit into the business if an individual wants to take it. It is likely that not all junior auditors will want to make a career in internal audit so it is important that it is seen to offer a route to business management positions." (British BAG Survey respondent)

The market for Internal Audit in Europe is a growing one. There are a series of factors that contribute to increasing the dynamism of the internal audit market:
- the unsecured environment (see the recent crisis) and the pressure of regulatory constraints
- the awareness of Executive management of the need to adopt a strong and efficient internal control system
- a market context where demand outstrips supply, which is additionally short, as numbers of "baby boomers" reach retirement age.

As a consequence, Internal Audit is an attractive career opportunity for young executives. In addition, the internal auditor in a bank is in a privileged position, because being prepared for larger operational responsibilities and business management positions. Internal audit also offers a complete and in-depth vision of the businesses, and develops the capacity for judgment and relationship skills.

However, as André Levy Lang, former head of Paribas, made plain in the media after the "Kerviel fraud", the salary differentials between traders and auditors are too great. Indeed, the level of salary on offer to internal auditors is not high enough to attract and retain high potential profiles.

As a consequence, it is important to acknowledge and to increase the standing of the internal audit function within and outside the banking organisation:
- Outside the organisation, it is the role of the IIA and its local chapters to represent the internal audit function, to promote its development and to disseminate the best practice.

– Raising the standing of the auditing function within the bank implies:
   - positioning the function at the top level of the organisation
   - interesting roles for auditors, their incentives being the variety and type of assignment, including both assurance and advisory aspects
   - acknowledgement of auditing as a discipline of management, and
   - above all, attractive offers of professional mobility for internal auditors leaving the function.

We therefore feel that an efficient audit team should be made up of:

1. young executives who spend a few years "learning" how the group operates and establishing a top management network that can be useful when seeking future career opportunities within the bank.
2. young executives (often from External Audit firms) who want to make a career within Internal Audit.
3. senior executives who "end" their career in Internal Audit by putting their operational experience to good use, whilst learning the new professional skills of Internal Audit.

**Banking Advisory Group Position on the Banking Internal Auditors
Profile and Career path**

Due to increasing regulatory requirements, to more demanding standards, to increasingly complex businesses/activities, banking organisations look for high potential internal auditors who have the necessary technical skills and a sound level of judgement.

According to the Banking Advisory Group, an efficient internal audit team is a combination of:
– experienced professionals with several years of practice in banking and/or audit, able to transmit their knowledge to new comers
– "young seniors" who have successful experience of at least two jobs and have demonstrated high potential
– specialised and generalist profiles
– "young executives" who become familiar with the Organisation's processes before taking high level positions within the bank (Internal Auditing as a discipline of management).

Each organisation needs to determine its optimum mix, as the needs of a retail bank are clearly different from those of an investment bank.

However, although current trends in the Audit market apparently enhance its attractiveness, the banking organisations will need to offer incentives and salaries that are motivating, if they wish to attract those with the best profiles.

Conclusion

The field of European Internal Auditing is a living one, continuously evolving in the twin directions of the building of the European financial market and of strengthening the role of audit within the Organisation.

In this context, the BAG supports the following principles:
– increasing the cooperation between national supervisors, as the first step toward European Banking supervision
– enhancing Audit Committee duties
– strengthening the independence of Internal Audit, which implies stronger links with the Audit Committee or Board
– promoting and developing the professionalism of the audit function
– implementing efficient coordination with the other control bodies.

These bodies should work towards the achievement of an ultimate goal, which is the better management of risks and an optimal framework for Corporate Governance.

The audit teams of the banks should anticipate the process leading towards the creation of a "European bank" by integrating, or at least by coordinating their actions, and adopting the same references and Standards, taking into account cultural diversity and local regulations. In so doing, Internal Audit will make its contribution to helping the banking sector reach its European objectives. This is the clearly stated and main goal of the Banking Advisory Group.

Appendices

Appendix 1: ECIIA B.A.G. Survey Questionnaire

1. What are the specific banking regulations (laws, Standards) on Internal Audit and Control in your country? What is the role assigned to Internal Audit by these regulations?

2. Please indicate how and by whom is the implementation of these regulations supervised and managed in your country?

3. How is the internal control system organised in your organisation? Who are the main actors of the Internal Control system?

4. How is Internal Audit organised?

5. Is the audit function totally independent from the different operational entities (business lines / functions…)?

6. What is the reporting line of Internal Audit in the Organisation: linked to the CEO? Reporting to the Audit Committee? Reporting both to the Board and the Chief Executive Officer?

7. What is the scope of Internal Audit? Auditing of the efficiency of the permanent control? Advisory role? Regulatory controls? What are the trends?

8. What specific skills and competencies should an auditor have?

9. Does the audit function represent an attractive career opportunity for a young executive? How would you describe the market trend for this position?

10. How is the audit function positioned in your organisation, in regard to personal development? Is it a genuine "metier"? A privileged school of management? A favoured path to an international career?

Appendix 2: Countries participating in the project

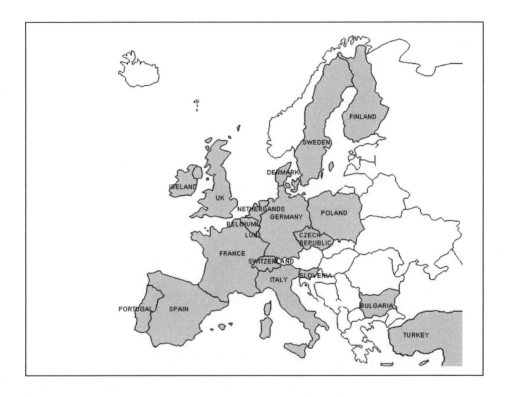

Figure 16: Map of the 18 European countries participating in the project.

Appendix 3: Representation of the CBOK Respondents of the Banking Sector by European Country

	Frequency	Percent
AUSTRIA	26	4.1%
BELGIUM	40	6.4%
BULGARIA	12	1.9%
CYPRUS	5	0.8%
CZECH REPUBLIC	40	6.4%
DENMARK	2	0.3%
ESTONIA	6	1.0%
FINLAND	6	1.0%
FRANCE	65	10.3%
GERMANY	40	6.4%
GREECE	23	3.7%
ITALY	141	22.4%
NETHERLANDS	50	7.9%
POLAND	17	2.7%
PORTUGAL	16	2.5%
ROMANIA	9	1.4%
SPAIN	59	9.4%
SWEDEN	14	2.2%
UNITED KINGDOM & IRELAND	58	9.2%

Figure 17: Representation of the CBOK respondents of the banking sector by European country.

Appendix 4: Scope of the Quality Assurance Review (QAR)

The Scope of the QAR can be divided into two parts.

The first of the two parts of a QAR programme focuses on the components of the management of an internal audit activity. This involves checks that internal auditing has all the requisite elements in place for conducting internal audit activities, including procedures, a formalised organisation, and sufficient and qualified staff.

The following aspects should be reviewed:
- the charter of internal audit activity
- the control environment of the audit practice and the positioning of the CAE within the organisation
- the audit plan, in order to ensure that the internal audit activity focuses on enterprise risk management, control, and governance processes and aligns its audit plans to the objectives of the organisation
- the range of knowledge, experience and skills within the internal audit team

However, even although an internal audit department may respect all the IIA Standards, this does not necessarily mean that the internal audit is satisfactory, nor that it brings value to the organisation. Hence the second part to the framework.

The second part of the quality assessment framework focuses on the expectations in respect of internal auditing, from the major groups involved in the governance process within an organisation.

There are four major groups involved:
- The **Oversight group**, comprising the Board of directors and its various committees.
- The **Stewardship group**, which is Executive management. This group has a dual role of stewardship (of the resources allocated by the Board) and of accountability for the results of the operations of the entire organisation
- The **Performance group,** which consists of operating and support management and staff. Their role is primarily that of delivering goods and services at expected levels of cost, within the time and resources allocated by executive management

- The **Assurance group,** whose role is to provide independent and objective assurance to the first three groups. It also provides advice and assistance; so as to enhance the Organisation's effectiveness.

This second part of the Quality Assistance Review consists of checking that Internal Audit, with all the ingredients and components available to it to perform its business, is actually efficient and an appropriate response to clients' needs. During a QAR, members from the four beneficiary groups are interviewed in order to assess how they perceive the internal audit department's work and how they feel it could be improved. We find this part of the work very interesting and challenging. It is easier to check compliance with the Standards than it is to check the real impact of Internal Audit on the organisation. Only independent reviewers can gather the true feelings and perceptions of the clients of internal audit.

Appendix 5: IIA Standards

1000 – Purpose, Authority, and Responsibility
The purpose, authority, and responsibility of the internal audit activity should be formally defined in a charter, consistent with the *Standards*, and approved by the board.

1100 – Independence and Objectivity
The internal audit activity should be independent, and internal auditors should be objective in performing their work.

1200 – Proficiency and Due Professional Care
Engagements should be performed with proficiency and due professional care.

1300 – Quality Assurance and Improvement Program
The chief audit executive should develop and maintain a quality assurance and improvement program that covers all aspects of the internal audit activity and continuously monitors its effectiveness. This program includes periodic internal and external quality assessments and ongoing internal monitoring. Each part of the program should be designed to help the internal auditing activity add value and improve the organization's operations and to provide assurance that the internal audit activity is in conformity with the *Standards* and the *Code of Ethics*.

2000 – Managing the Internal Audit Activity
The chief audit executive should effectively manage the internal audit activity to ensure it adds value to the organization.

2100 – Nature of Work
The internal audit activity should evaluate and contribute to the improvement of risk management, control, and governance processes using a systematic and disciplined approach.

2200 – Engagement Planning
Internal auditors should develop and record a plan for each engagement, including the scope, objectives, timing and resource allocations.

2300 – Performing the Engagement
Internal auditors should identify, analyze, evaluate, and record sufficient information to achieve the engagement's objectives.

2400 – Communicating Results
Internal auditors should communicate the engagement results.

2500 – Monitoring Progress
The chief audit executive should establish and maintain a system to monitor the disposition of results communicated to management.

2600 – Resolution of Management's Acceptance of Risks
When the chief audit executive believes that senior management has accepted a level of residual risk that may be unacceptable to the organization, the chief audit executive should discuss the matter with senior management. If the decision regarding residual risk is not resolved, the chief audit executive and senior management should report the matter to the board for resolution.

Appendix 6: Basel Committee Principles from "Internal Audits in Banks and Supervisor's Relationships with Auditors" (August 2001, updated in August 2002)

Principle 1

The bank's board of directors has the ultimate responsibility for ensuring that senior management establishes and maintains an adequate and effective system of internal controls, a measurement system for assessing the various risks of the bank's activities, a system for relating risks to the bank's capital level, and appropriate methods for monitoring compliance with laws, regulations, and supervisory and internal policies. At least once a year, the board of directors should review the internal control system and the capital assessment procedure.

Principle 2

The bank's senior management is responsible for developing processes that identify measure, monitor and control risks incurred by the bank. At least once a year, senior management should report to the board of directors on the scope and performance of the internal control system and of the capital assessment procedure.

Principle 3

Internal audit is part of the ongoing monitoring of the bank's system of internal controls and of its internal capital assessment procedure, because internal audit provides an independent assessment of the adequacy of, and compliance with, the bank's established policies and procedures. As such, the internal audit function assists senior management and the board of directors in the efficient and effective discharge of their responsibilities as described above.

Principle 4

Each bank should have a permanent internal audit function. In fulfilling its duties and responsibilities, the senior management should take all necessary measures so that the bank can continuously rely on an adequate internal audit function appropriate to its size and to the nature of its operations. These measures include providing the appropriate resources and staffing to internal audit to achieve its objectives.

Principle 5
The bank's internal audit function must be independent of the activities audited and must also be independent from the every day internal control process. This means that internal audit is given an appropriate standing within the bank and carries out its assignments with objectivity and impartiality.

Principle 6
Each bank should have an internal audit charter that enhances the standing and authority of the internal audit function within the bank.

Principle 7
The internal audit function should be objective and impartial, which means it should be in a position to perform its assignments free from bias and interference.

Principle 8
The professional competence of every internal auditor and of the internal audit function as a whole is essential for the proper functioning of the bank's internal audit function.

Principle 9
Every activity and every entity of the bank should fall within the scope of the internal audit.

Principle 10
Within the framework of the bank's internal capital assessment process, internal audit should carry out regularly an independent review of the risk management system developed by the bank to relate risk to the bank's capital level and the method established for monitoring compliance with internal capital policies.

Principle 11
Internal audit includes drawing up an audit plan, examining and assessing the available information, communicating the results, and following up recommendations and issues.

Principle 12
The head of the internal audit department should be responsible for ensuring that the department complies with sound internal auditing principles.

Principle 13
Bank supervisors should evaluate the work of the bank's internal audit department and, if satisfied, can rely on it to identify areas of potential risk.

Principle 14

Supervisory authorities should have periodic consultations with the bank's internal auditors to discuss the risk areas identified and the measures taken. At the same occasion, the extent of the collaboration between the bank's internal audit department and the bank's external auditors may also be discussed.

Principle 15

Supervisors are encouraged to arrange regular discussions of policy issues jointly with the heads of internal audit departments of the banks under their supervision.

Principle 16

Supervisory authorities should encourage consultation between internal and external auditors in order to make their cooperation as efficient and effective as possible.

Principle 17

Work performed for a bank's supervisory authority by an external auditor should have a legal or contractual basis. Any task assigned by the supervisory authority to the external auditor should be complementary to his/her regular audit work and should be within his/her competence.

Principle 18

Cooperation among the supervisor, the external auditor and the internal auditor aims to make the work of all concerned parties more efficient and effective. The cooperation may be based on periodic meetings of the supervisor, the external auditor and internal auditor.

Principle 19

The creation of a permanent audit committee is a solution to meet the practical difficulties that may arise from the board of directors' task to ensure the existence and maintenance of an adequate system of controls. In addition, such a committee reinforces the internal control system and the internal and external audit. Therefore, banks are encouraged to set up a permanent audit committee, especially if they are involved in complex activities. Banks' subsidiaries should also consider the appropriateness of setting up an audit committee within their board of directors.

Principle 20

Regardless of whether internal audit activities are outsourced, the board of directors and senior management remain ultimately responsible for ensuring that the system of internal control and the internal audit are adequate and operate effectively.

Appendix 7: BAG Survey completed Questionnaires by Country

Question 1: What are the specific banking regulations (laws, Standards) on internal audit and control in your country? What is the role assigned to internal audit by these regulations?	
Belgium	A specific circular on Internal Audit has been issued by the Banking Commission in Belgium. Circular D1 97/4 specifies requirements governing the Internal Audit profession. Other legislative enactments mention Internal Audit and its relationship to external auditors, to the Compliance department, and to risk management (PPB‑2007‑6‑CPB‑CPA (Good governance). D1 2001/13 covers the Compliance department, and D1 99/2 the synergy between external auditors and Internal Audit. The role assigned to Internal Audit is difficult to encapsulate, but the following is the definition given by the law: "Internal Audit is an independent function responsible for assessing the internal control environment, and its efficiency and adequacy."
Bulgaria	Bank Supervision Ordinance No. 10 is dedicated to Internal Control in Banks, and determines the requirements laid upon the internal control system in banks and banking groups. It describes internal audit as an independent part of the internal control system, so providing an assurance of due process in banking operations and control systems. Ordinance No. 10 lays down the general requirements governing the internal audit function, including its set up and scope of work, reporting, and relations with supervisory authorities. It also requires compliance by internal audit to Standards on Internal Auditing. A number of other regulations address the issue of the soundness of the internal audit function, as a means for assisting the stability of banking operations. Internal audit is required to notify the Banking Supervision Department in the Bulgarian National Bank, of any such violations or malpractice affecting the bank's management, as have led or may lead to material damages.
Czech Republic	The banks in the Czech Republic are obliged under banking law to set up an internal audit function. Banks are encouraged to follow IIA Standards.
Denmark	Internal audit is regulated by the Executive Order on Auditing, which lays down extensive obligations regarding roles and responsibilities, etc.
Finland (3 respondents) *Questionnaire 1:*	The Financial Supervision Authority set up under Finland's regulatory paper on Corporate Governance and Business Activity, covers both internal control and internal audit, alongside other governance issues. It builds on a set of corporate government standards and guideline issued by the OECD and Basel Committee on Banking Supervision. It is also aligned with IIA Standards. Internal audit is an activity independent from any other activities, in order to provide an assurance of the effectiveness of internal control.

Finland	Questionnaire 2:	FSA standards regulate the internal control and internal audit functions. These standards follow IIA standards. Internal audit plays its role independently of other departments, and its duties are specified by IIA.
	Questionnaire 3:	As a multilateral institution, we have tried to follow the best available market practice. Internal audit work is performed in accordance with International standards for professional practice in this field, issued by the Institute of Internal Auditors.
France		The French banks are aligned with IIA Standards. They follow the recommendations of the Basel Committee. Locally, French banks follow the rules of the CRBF (Comité de la Réglementation bancaire et financière – Committee for Banking and Financial Regulation) 97–02. Each credit institution is required to set up an adequate internal control environment by adapting the systems required under this Regulation to the nature and volume of their activities, their size, their establishments and to the various types of risk to which they are exposed. Internal control procedures require in particular that the following be in place: – Control system for operations and internal procedures; – Appropriately organized accounting and information processing system; – Risk and results measurement system; – Risk monitoring and control systems; – Documentation and information system. CRBF 97–02 has been supplemented several times since it was first published. The main decrees were issued as 2001–01, 2004–02, 2005–03 and 2007–07. Market-listed French banks are governed by the French Financial Security Act which states that they are required to give an account „…" of the internal control procedures that the company has implemented," that duty devolving on the Chairman of the Board of Directors or of the Supervisory Board. The rules issued by the Autorité des Marchés Financiers (AMF – Financial Markets Authority) apply on a mandatory basis to asset management activities, and may be applied more extensively. There are also several professional bodies, such as the European Banking Federation and the French Banking Federation which represent the interests of banks. They exchange best practice, discuss legislative proposals and initiatives, and adopt common positions. The roles of Internal Audit as defined by the IIA standards is to add value and improve the organization's operations by performing its roles (including consultancy) independently, providing an assurance of objectiveness, so helping the organization achieving its objectives by driving a systematic, disciplined approach to evaluate and improve the effectiveness of risk management, of controls, and of the governance process. It also carries out periodic control of the compliance of operations and procedures, assessing the level of risk actually incurred, and of the effectiveness and appropriateness of the Permanent Control System.

Germany	Internal Audit is regulated by law (KWG – German Banking Act) and by the MaRisk, the German minimum requirements for Risk Management in banking organizations issued by BaFin, the German regulator. (For more detail please refer to the information already received).
Italy	**Role of Internal Audit in banking organizations** In 1999, the Italian banking authority, Bank of Italy, relying on the Italian banking law ("Testo Unico Bancario", issued in 1993), issued specific regulations ("Istruzioni di Vigilanza per le Banche") aiming at defining a specifically disciplined approach to corporate governance in banking organizations, including administrative and accounting procedures and internal control systems. In the regulatory text, specific attention is attached to the role, the objectives and the activities of the internal audit function, which is regarded as the top ("third layer") of the control framework adopted. From a regulatory perspective, the Internal audit function plays an important, primary role of "assurance" of the proper functioning of the internal control system, which should be kept under continuous supervision, backed up by on-site control assignments. Internal Audit is given the mandate of performing general compliance and risk monitoring, extending to IT systems and to foreign branches, supported by a direct reporting line to the board and top management, for the purposes of improving risk management policies, measurement tools and procedures. The control framework for banking regulation is presently undergoing an in-depth review process in view of the forthcoming introduction into the Italian system of the compliance function, under the Basel Committee's guidelines. CONSOB, the Italian Securities and Financial Market Commission, issued specific regulations covering the internal control function of investment services. The Authority for Italian Financial Markets, basing itself on the law on investment services ("Testo Unico della Finanza", issued in 1998 and amended in 2007), has established a specific regulation requiring banking organizations operating investment services to set up an internal control function. The mandate of the internal control function sets objectives in the field of "assurance", including procedures and a control system assessing the performance of investment services (i.e. monitoring clients' complaints procedures), and in the field of "consulting" services, including regulation and behavioural issues, with specific recommendations on conflicts of interest. Both Bank of Italy and Consob regulations regard internal audit as an independent function within the organization, endowed with full rights of access to company files and information. According to Bank of Italy rules, the mandate of internal audit and attached responsibilities must be set out in an audit charter approved by the Board. The profile of the audit function must be consistent with the following principles:

| Italy | – Independence;
– Adequate quality and size of staff;
– Full access to all corporate information and activities, even when outsourced;
Consob lays down that the internal control function should be endowed with organizational independence and perform its work autonomously and objectively.

Due to changes in the regulatory framework, which cover the compliance function, and in response to the MIFID Directive, the Italian regulations on investment services and the mandate of the internal control function, have been significantly modified. In particular, the internal control function has been replaced by two levels of control introduced by the MiFID regulation: compliance and internal audit. Moreover, in term of self-regulation, the Code of Conduct for listed companies published by the Italian Stock Exchange, requires the organization to set an internal audit function which has to be independent, adequately staffed and able to obtain necessary information.

Linkage of Internal Auditing to the Corporate Governance structure
Bank of Italy regulations require that complete and continuous reporting be provided by internal audit to all actors involved in corporate governance (Board, Collegio Sindacale, senior management), on a regular basis

In the Consob framework, the direct reporting line from the control functions (compliance, internal audit), in regard to the annual plan, findings and complaints analysis, is currently under review. The regulation sets down procedures for annual reporting from those functions to the Board and Collegio Sindacale.

Unlike Consob, Bank of Italy does not require a direct reporting line from the audit function (as specified above), but prompt information from the Collegio Sindacale and external auditors, in cases of serious breach to regulations or management failure.

In terms of general principles of good corporate governance, the Italian Stock Exchange, in the Code of Conduct for listed companies (including banks), requires companies to set up an internal audit function, whose responsibility it is (cf. "preposto al controllo interno") to guarantee adequate information to the Audit Committee (if any) and to the Collegio Sindacale, about proper and effective risk management and internal control system operations. An Audit Committee is not specifically required by the current Italian regulatory framework, but is an important part of the self-regulatory framework. The Italian Stock Exchange, in the code of conduct for listed companies, regards the Audit Committee as providing "best practice" in the field of corporate governance. The Committee should be made up of non-executive directors, mainly independent |

Italy	The Code is adopted by listed companies on a voluntary basis. In case of adoption, relevant information must be supplied under the annual reporting format (according to the "comply or explain" rule). Consob has supervision powers over the effective implementation of such official disclosures, as laid down by recent regulations (n.262/05, "Law on Public savings and financial markets") The Bank of Italy's regulation allows banks to outsource internal audits. The right to total outsourcing is limited to smaller banks, subject to the responsibility and control of the Board. Outsourcing should be formalized in a contract with specific guarantees and service level standards. All banking organizations can outsource specific audit services in order to assure particular professional skills. In both cases, prior information to the Bank of Italy has to be supplied.
Luxembourg	Banking regulation: CSSF circular 98/143 modified by circular CSSF 04/0155 on internal control and CSSF circular 96/126 on administrative organization. CSSF Circular 98/143 defines four levels of control in the Bank: – Daily controls performed by executing employees whose aim is to quickly detect errors or omissions affecting operations, – Permanent critical control performed by persons in charge of administrative tasks. That control is ensured only if the segregation of duties is respected, as between operations execution and operations control, involving hierarchical controls, validation in order to respect the delegation of powers from Senior Management, internal limitations on powers devolved, the four eyes principle, etc. – Senior Management control over entities under their direct responsibility: budgets, profitability, compliance to caps on risk exposure.... – Internal audit control, whose role is to assess the whole of the banks' internal control environment and so assist Senior Management in gaining better control over its business operations. – The scope of internal audit should extend to all activities and functions of the credit institution or FSP (Financial Sector Professional). In performing its work, the internal audit department should make reference to CSSF regulations and recommendations. – The internal audit department should determine whether:

Luxembourg	• The system for the identification, measurement and control of risks is operating satisfactorily;
	• Securities and other assets are being properly administrated;
	• Transactions are being correctly executed;
	• Transactions are being completely and accurately recorded and reliably and promptly reported;
	• Company operations and organization comply with relevant rules and regulations;
	• Decisions made by Management and by those duly authorized by it, are put into action and established procedures for the conduct of banking business or applicable to the FSP, are complied with
	− The scope of the internal audit department of the Luxembourg institution should be extended to the foreign branches and to subsidiaries, both in Luxembourg and abroad. The internal audit department should make regular site visits to branches. The internal audit departments at branch level (if any) should be subordinate to the head−office audit department and report to it. Significant branches should have their own local audit department, and should respect the provisions of CSSF circular 98/143.
	The internal auditors should be permanently based in the organization and the audit plan should cover the period under review and the way the audit plan is effectively implemented. Full outsourcing of the audit activity to a third party may be authorized by the CSSF for small banks and where the activity risk profile is low.
	The requirement for objectivity lays down that internal auditors avoid conflicts of interest:
	− The rotation of internal auditors should be planned to ensure that controls are not performed continuously by the same auditor;
	− Internally recruited internal auditors should audit activities or functions they did not previously perform in operational departments of the organization.
	Internal auditors should not design or implement any organizational measures.
	Internal Audit must be independent from the entities that it audits and must not depend of another service of the bank, but must be directly report to Senior executives. The person in charge of Internal Audit must be able to have direct access to the President of the Board of Directors, to the President of the Audit Committee, and to external auditors.

Luxembourg	All the objectives, duties and protection of Internal Audits are defined in the Audit Charter. In-service training should be available to audit staff. If the internal audit department is not sufficiently competent in a particular area and uses the services of an external specialist, the external expert should work under the supervision of the head of the internal audit department and report directly to that person. The expert should be independent of the organization's statutory auditor. To ensure the promptest possible detection of errors or omissions in routine tasks, the system of internal control should provide for daily performed controls by operators over transactions. The system of internal control should fulfil the following three objectives: 1. The internal control system should be based on central administration principles (LMI Circular 95/120) and on accounting and administrative organization (LMI Circular 96/126). 2. The system of internal control should have an appropriate mechanism for the identification, measurement, control and reporting of risks from a financial and an operational point of view. 3. The system should have an internal audit function.
Netherlands	The Law on Financial Supervision, enacted as of 1 January 2007, serves as the basis for the regulations to be adhered to by the banking sector. These are elaborated further in decrees. Internal audit plays a prominent role in safeguarding the sound operations of the bank. The law requires a bank to have in place an internal audit function.
Poland	The basic regulation which defines the role of internal audit and internal controls is the banking law which came into force on 1 May 2004. According to the law: – In banks, the internal controls should be in place. The purpose of internal controls is to assist the decision-making processes and hence ensure: (i) the effectiveness and efficiency of banking operations (ii) the reliability of financial information (iii) compliance to laws and internal policies. The bank's management board is responsible for designing, implementing and operating internal controls. – The bank's supervisory board oversees the implementation of internal controls and assesses their adequacy and effectiveness.

Poland	– Banks when incorporated as joint stock companies, state-owned companies and cooperative companies should have an internal audit unit. The purpose of internal audit is to test and assess, in an independent and objective way, the adequacy and effectiveness of internal controls and also to express opinions with respect to the management of the bank, including its risk management. Information on findings, irregularities, conclusions and the recommendations arising from audits, should be periodically communicated to the supervisory board.
	– The supervisory board may appoint from among its members, the audit committee which supervises the activity of internal audit unit.
	– Internal auditing may not be outsourced. The supervisory board is obliged to inform the Supervisory Banking Commission about the members of the management board to whom the internal audit unit reports.
	The statute of a bank should describe the principles of the internal controls system in operation.
	Over and above the general banking law, the Polish Banking Supervisory Commission introduced in the 2007 regulation, addresses the issue of the Basel Committee New Capital Adequacy requirements. These regulations also specify requirements regarding internal controls and internal audit:
	– The management board of a bank should ensure that operations performed for the purposes of internal auditing meet the requirement of banking law, i.e. that they:
	Cover the operations of the bank as a whole;
	Are consistent with the IAD charter, which specifies the purpose, scope and detailed principles of operations and organizational structure of IAD, and are based on a written auditing methodology;
	Are performed under appropriate and written methods regarding sampling;
	Have the scope and frequency determined in audit plans and are adequate to identified risks and their materiality;
	Are adequately documented;
	Assess the effectiveness of the implementation of the recommendations issued by IAD.
	– The Management Board of a bank should ensure that there is proper cooperation by all the bank's employees with IAD, and that there is access for auditors to source evidence, including confidential information, so ensuring the effectiveness and continuity of IAD operations.
	– The Management Board should ensure that audit operations are performed by competent, qualified and experienced staff to test the risk inherent in the bank's operations.
	– The bank should set up mechanisms to ensure the independence of IAD, in particular:

Poland	• The IAD manager should have direct access to the President of the bank's management board and supervisory board;
	• There should be a detailed process/mode of hiring and dismissing the IAD manager;
	• There should be a detailed process/mode of control of the levels of compensation of the IAD manager and staff;
	• The IAD manager should participate in meetings of the Management Board and Supervisory Board, if there are issues related to IAD operations (responsibilities relating to, or supervision of IAD);
	• The IAD manager should participate at least annually in the Supervisory Board meetings, whenever IAD operations are discussed;
	• Provide protection for IAD staff against dismissal.
	– Based on IAD operations, reports to the management board and supervisory reports should be provided with current and detailed information, sourced from IAD reports, on:
	• Compliance to legal and other requirements, and to internal regulations;
	• Risk management and the Management information system;
	• The effectiveness of internal controls in bringing to light mistakes and irregularities, and on the effectiveness of mitigation steps/action plans;
	• Execution of the bank's objectives and policies, as determined and required by management;
	• The completeness, regularity and comprehensiveness of the bank's accounting procedures
	• Quality (accuracy and reliability) of systems: accounting, reporting and operational
	– The adequacy, functionality and security of IT systems.
	– The effectiveness of the use of means/financial resources including funds and resources regarding all the bank's operations.
	– Assessment of the bank's organizational structure, segregation of duties and coordination of activities among individual organizational units and positions, as well as the preparation and flow of documents.
	– Assessment of internal systems regarding the efficiency of the bank's operations.
	– Outsourced activities.
	– Art 38. The president of the management board is responsible for taking decisions regarding the use of the results of the internal auditing process and for informing audited units about such decisions. The audited unit should then provide IAD with information on the deadlines and results of mitigation action plans.

Poland	Over and above banking law and Banking Supervisory Commission regulations, the Banking Supervisory Commission from time to time issues recommendations regarding the bank's best practices and regulatory expectations. These also cover expectations from the internal audit function, i.e.: – Recommendation „B" (2002) on "Limiting the risk of the banks' financial investments". Internal Audit should perform tests and reviews regarding the correctness of valuations of securities, contributions, shares and derivatives, in the light of appropriate evidence. – Recommendation „C" (2002) on "Management of credit concentration risk". In Internal Audit reports dedicated to this area, there should be specially dedicated sections to discuss the concentration risk affecting banks in regard to their assets, liabilities, and off-balance liabilities – Recommendation „D" (2002) on "Management of risks related to IT and telecommunications systems". The role and objectives of Internal audit in this area are defined as the testing and review of the risk management process related to IT risk, thereby assessing potential threats and ensuring the adequate security of assets/ resources, for the purposes of judging whether controls in this area are effective and efficient. The IT audit should be based on widely recognized standards (COBIT, ISACA standards, COSO).The bank's management is responsible for setting up the IT Audit function. – Recommendation „G" (2002) on "Interest rate risk management in banks". Internal Audit should test whether procedures and policies are followed by the persons involved in the management of interest rate risk, and assess whether these procedures ensure that objectives will be met. The periodical review and assessment of the interest rate risk management process may be performed by the internal audit department, unless the internal auditors have knowledge, not only of audit procedures, but also enough expertise on interest rate risk management. – Recommendation „H" (2002) on "Guidelines regarding internal controls and internal audit within banks". The document discusses: (i) differences between internal controls and internal audit, and their objectives, scope, responsibility, (ii) components of the internal control system: control environment, risk assessment, control activities, information and communication, monitoring, (iii) internal audit unit responsibilities and organization: the place in the organization, responsibilities, rights, scope of activity, the areas of focus by internal audit, internal audit charter & procedures, the need for constant training and development, the need to employ consultants, planning of audit assignments and their execution, the communication of audit results, internal audit in branches (if applicable), cooperation with regulator(s) and external auditors (iv) the list of issues to be reviewed by regulators during their examinations, in regard to internal controls and internal audit, (v) basic terms relating to internal controls and auditing (vi) code of ethics.

Poland	– Recommendation „L" (2001) on "The role of External Auditors in the supervision of a bank". The need of co-operation between the external and internal auditors is highlighted, as a means to increasing the efficiency and effectiveness of the work of the external auditors. There should be direct contact between and informa-tion exchange among external auditors, regulators and internal auditors. These three parties should meet together (i) to discuss the results of examinations performed by regulators, (ii) after the bank's financial statements have been approved, (iii) in other important cases, i.e. when decisions about mergers are taken.
	– Recommendation „M" (2004) on "Operational Risk Management in banks". The periodical reviews and as-sessments of operational risk management should be performed by internal audit. Internal audit should be connected to risk management. However, it should be highlighted that internal audit cannot be responsible for risk management. Internal audit should provide for the objective assessment of the efficiency, adequacy and effectiveness of the management and quality of operations. Internal audit should especially focus on operational risks connected with new products entering new markets, owing to the fact that recently many banks have suffered losses in such areas of business.
	– Recommendation „P" (2002) on "Monitoring system for financial liquidity in banks". The purpose of internal audit with regard to the monitoring and management of liquidity should give rise to discussion and action. For instance: it should be ensured that established procedures and policies are followed by every unit of the bank, that reviews are made of the adequacy of procedures, that there are reviews of the adequacy of established limits; that there is an assurance that the information used for the management of liquidity is reliable and up to date; that checks are made of the implementation of if the recommendations from previ-ous audits.
	– Recommendation „R" (2006) on "Identification of impaired in-balance credit exposures, and determination of the level of reserves for off-balance credit exposures". Banks should describe their audit procedures taking the form of reviews and tests. Audits in this area should be performed at least every two years. The scope of audit should cover: the adequacy of credit risk management, taking into account the complexity/range of the bank's operations, and the completeness and accuracy of data and parameters.

Portugal	Bank of Portugal is the regulatory body overseeing the banking industry in Portugal. There are specific regulations concerning internal control systems in financial institutions. These should include the definition of organizational structures and the methods and procedures in place to achieve the objectives of internal control and minimize financial, operational, and legal and reputation risks. There are no specific regulations governing the internal audit function. However, the internal control regulation states that the internal audit function in financial institutions should be adequate to the scale and nature of the activities developed, and include the monitoring both of the efficiency and adequacy of internal controls, and of compliance to internal rules and procedures, whilst ensuring the accuracy and timeliness of the information produced.
Slovenia	The rules on internal audit and control that apply to banks only, are contained in the Banking Act. However, the banks also apply „general" rules in the field, as contained in the Standards of professional conduct for internal auditing, in the Code of principles of internal audit and in the Code of ethics of internal auditors.
Sweden (2 respondents) *Questionnaire 1:*	There are no legal requirements. The Swedish FSA directive however does require the banks to set up an Internal Audit Function.
Questionnaire 2:	With our Head Office based in Stockholm, Sweden, the Bank as a whole is governed by the rules and regulations stipulated by the Finansinspection (the Swedish Financial Supervisory Authority) and the Swedish Bankers Association. Local branches and subsidiaries must also abide by the rules and regulations set by their local regulator. Our group-wide Group Audit Methodology (GAM) brings together a cohesive set of guidelines, originating both in existing internal good practices as well as in external best practices. It is consistent with the Institute of Internal Auditors' (IIA) Professional Practices Framework and embeds the concepts of the COSO framework. The IIA Professional Practices Framework sets out clear guidelines for the internal audit department. The Finansinspection and the Swedish Bankers Association do not stipulate a role that differs from that defined by the IIA. According the regulation from the Swedish Finansinpection, Internal Audit shall act as the third line of defence and report directly to the Board. There are also specific requirements on Internal Audit in the Basel II and MiFid regulations.
Switzerland	The Banking regulations in Switzerland are essentially based on two authorities: – The Federal Banking Commission (FBC) which is the supervisory authority of the banks in Switzerland; – The Swiss Bankers Association which acts as a self-regulating agent. Internal audit is organized as per Swiss Federal Banking Commission circular 06/6 which sets guidelines for corporate governance, the supervision of business, internal control and internal audit. Internally, all procedures currently in force within our Group are also applicable.

Turkey	Turkish Banking Law, numbered 5411, is the main regulation for banks. Articles 29, 30, 31 and 32 are the main regulations. Banking Law in English can be found under legislation section of the English pages of BRSA's website (www.bddk.org.tr). Banking Law can also be accessed from the following link of the Turkish Banking Association, in English, on http://www.tbb.org.tr/english/5411.doc.
	Banking Regulation and Supervision Agency, the regulator, on November 1, 2006 published the Regulation on Internal Systems, which describes the roles and responsibilities of the Audit Committee, Internal Audit, Internal Control, Risk Management, the Compliance divisions and of senior management. Publicly traded banks in Istanbul Stock Exchange are also required to follow also regulations of the Capital Markets Board (www.cmb.gov.tr).
	Under this regulation, Internal Audit is responsible for giving an assurance to the Board on internal controls and risk management systems in the banks. Internal audit has also a consultancy role.
UK / Ireland	The FSA requires financial institutions to have an internal audit function where it is considered by the organization proportionate to do so. There is no requirement which lays down that a financial organization must have an internal audit function.
	The FSA requirements relating to internal audit are contained within the SYSC (Senior Management Arrangements, Systems and Controls) section 6.2. These state that Internal Audit has the following responsibilities:
	1. To establish, implement and maintain an audit plan to examine and evaluate the adequacy and effectiveness of the firm's systems, internal control mechanisms and arrangements;
	2. To issue recommendations based on the result of work carried out in accordance with (1);
	3. To verify compliance with those recommendations; and
	4. To report in relation to internal audit matters in accordance with SYSC Rule 4.3.2 (reporting to senior management).

Question 2: Please indicate how and by whom is the implementation of these regulations supervised and managed in your country?	
Belgium	The Belgian Banking Commission oversees the implementation of these regulations. There are also several professional bodies, such as the European Banking Federation and the Belgian Banking Federation, which represent the interests of banks, through exchanging best practices, debating legislative proposals and initiatives, and adopting common positions.
Bulgaria	The banking regulations are formally issued by the Central Bank Supervision Department before being adopted and implemented by the banking system. Laws governing the operation of the banking system are formally adopted by the National Assembly. Each year, individual paragraphs of the regulatory texts are amended and improved. Banking Supervision has an external monitoring function over the organization and efficiency of internal control systems in banks and banking groups. It ensures the free flow of communications with the internal audit departments, covering banking risks, the measures taken, as well as relations with the external auditors. The banks are reviewed on a regular basis for compliance with prudential banking requirements, through the issuance by the banking institutions of regular information/reports, discussions with management, and on-site examinations.
Czech Republic	The implementation of this obligation is supervised by the Czech National Bank (CNB). There are also professional bodies. The Czech Banking Association and its Internal Audit Committee represent the interests of banks through exchanging best practices, debating legislative and regulatory proposals, issuing recommendations for banks, etc. The Czech Institute of Internal Auditors supports exchanging best practices and adopting common positions in the internal audit area.
Denmark	The Financial Supervisory Authority issues laws and regulations for financial institutions and also undertakes the inspection of compliance.
Finland (3 respondents) Questionnaire 1:	The Financial Supervision Authority.
Questionnaire 2:	The Financial Supervision Authority supervises implementation. We also have the Federation of Finnish Financial Services representing the interests of banks and insurance companies.

Finland *Questionnaire 3:*	As a multilateral institution we are not under the supervision of any public authority. We have a special Control Committee appointed by our owners (the eight Member countries) who supervise us. The other Banks located in Finland are under the Finnish Financial Supervisory Authority.
France	In France the implementation of CRBF 97-02 is supervised by the Banking Commission and its role is defined by the Code monétaire et financier, as being: – Control of the respect by the credit institutions of the legal and regulatory measures applicable to them, including the application of sanctions as necessary. – Examination of working procedures and verification of financial soundness. – Verification of the rules of the professional good practice. The Financial Markets Authority (AMF) also verifies the compliance of the French banks to the rules relating to Asset Management activities.
Germany	The implementation of MaRisk regulations is monitored and supervised by BaFin, the sovereign body for German banking regulations. However, BaFin also employs the German Bundesbank as well as external audit firms, to perform operative monitoring and on-site assessment of the implementation of banking regulations. There are various means of performing supervisory tasks, i.e. the issuance by the banking institutions of regular information/reports, discussions with management, and on-site examinations. The larger institutions may also hold annual meetings with Internal Audit Management.
Italy	The Bank of Italy supervises the banks and financial institutions, reviewing their stability and organization. Consob supervises the correctness and methods of information disclosure. The Italian Banking Federation represents the interests of the banks, through exchanging best practice, debating legislative proposals and initiatives and adopting common positions.
Luxembourg	In Luxembourg, the CSSF is the sole authority in charge of the supervision of the Banks. In the field of Internal Controls, each bank must send to CSSF: – A report by the bank's senior management on the internal control situation, the purpose being to give a general assessment on internal controls, insufficiencies, corrective measures and follow-up of their implementation.

Luxembourg	– A copy of the summaries of all the assignments performed by Internal Audit during the year. In parallel, there are also several professional bodies, such as the ABBL (Association des Banques et Banquiers au Luxembourg) for the banks, and ALFI, the Association of the Investment Fund Industry, which represent the interests of banks, through exchanging best practices, debating legislative proposals and initiatives and adopting common positions.
Netherlands	In the Netherlands, the Dutch Central Bank (De Nederlandsche Banks) supervises the follow-up by the banks of the implementation of regulations and decrees. The Dutch Banking Federation (Nederlandse Vereniging van Banken), which represents the interests of banks, has several commissions in place. Best practice is exchanged on the deployment of banking activities, and positions are taken on how to best deal with common issues. Best practice is also being developed, amongst others by the Basel Committee on Banking Supervision.
Poland	In Poland, the Banking Act requires that banks shall set up an adequate internal control environment. The bank's management board is responsible for designing, implementing and operating internal controls, as it has oversight over the implementation of internal controls and assesses their adequacy and effectiveness. Internal Audit assesses, in an independent and objective way, the adequacy and effectiveness of internal controls and also expresses its opinion with respect to the management of the bank, including risk management. The Polish Banking Supervision Commission controls the implementation of this regulation. The Polish Banking Association represents the interests of the banks, through exchanging best practices, debating legislative proposals and initiatives and adopting common positions. The implementation of and compliance to these regulations is supervised by the Bank of Portugal through its supervisory arm.

Slovenia	Under the Banking Act, internal audit comprises: 1. Monitoring and assessing the efficacy of risk management systems and providing assistance in risk management; 2. Review, assessment and testing the effectiveness of internal control systems; 3. Evaluating the process of assessing the necessary core capital regarding the bank's risk exposure, as assessed; 4. Assessing the reliability of the information system, including the electronic information system and electronic banking services; 5. Assessing the accuracy and reliability of accounting records and financial reports; 6. Verifying the completeness, reliability and timeliness of reporting in compliance with regulations; 7. Verifying the compliance of the bank's operations to regulations, internal rules and the resulting measures adopted; 8. Conducting special investigations.
Sweden (2 respondents) *Questionnaire 1:*	Swedish FSA (See other questions).
Questionnaire 2:	The Audit Committee has overall responsibility for the internal audit department. The External Auditors, employed by the audit committee, may also at times evaluate the work performed by the internal audit team. We are in the process of establishing a quality assurance program in 2008, which will monitor our adherence to both the IIA standards and the GAM process. In December 2006, we undertook a self assessment with external validation (Big Four validation).
Switzerland	In Switzerland, control is organized as per Swiss Federal Banking Commission circular 06/6, which sets guidelines for corporate governance, for the supervision of business and for internal control. The external auditors (acting on behalf of the regulators) control the application of this guideline.
Turkey	The Banking Regulation and Supervision Agency is the sole regulator. On www.bddk.org.tr, the mission and roles of BRSA can be accessed in English.
UK / Ireland	The regulations are enforced by the FSA. The FSA undertakes an "Arrow" review of each financial institution, over a 1 to 3 year period, depending upon the risk profile of the organization. During the Arrow review, the work of internal Audit is reviewed in detail.

Question 3:
How is the internal control system organized in your organization? Who are the main actors of the internal control system?

Belgium	The internal control system is organized on different levels: 1. The Compliance department is responsible for Compliance matters; 2. The Sales Control and Coaching Team is responsible for the "second line" control. They check transactions and files received from the sales network; 3. The Operations and MIS control department performs controls on day-to-day operations; 4. Different Committees discuss issues, risks and controls, compliance matters, etc. These are organized on a monthly/quarterly basis; 5. We have implemented a RCSA system (Risk & Control Self-Assessment). Each Quarter, important risks and controls are assessed and tested by each unit within the bank (departments and sub-departments). Senior Management and Line Management are responsible for implementing processes and controls. Apart from the above, we also have an independent Internal Audit department in Belgium (see below). Finally, we have the Group Audit (independent from any business around the world and reporting to New York HQ).
Bulgaria	Bank management generally seeks a reasonable level of controls. The internal control system corresponds to the size and the nature of the banking organization. The internal control system in banks encompasses management controls (establishment of policies and procedures, delegation of responsibilities, risk management policies and other), as well as risk identification, assessment, management and reporting, and, more generally, information and reporting. Executive management is the main actor involved in creating, assessing and monitoring the internal control system. Internal audit in the banking sector is an integral part of the internal control system, and its role is to support management in the process of its assessment of the internal control system.
Czech Republic	The purpose, authority and responsibility of the internal audit in our bank, its position within the internal control system and its relation to the external auditor, are governed by the our bank's internal regulations (Guideline for the Performance of the Internal Audit, Guideline for the Specification of Principles and Performance of the internal control). The internal control system is an integral part of the bank's organization and management. It includes all types of control, both preventive and ongoing as well as detective. These controls should provide a sufficient assurance that: – The goals are attained and tasks completed; – Resources are used effectively and efficiently;

Czech Republic	– Adequate controls are in place for the risks to which the relevant activities are exposed; cf. point 7); – Assets are safeguarded; – Financial and management information is reliable and possesses integrity; and – Actions and decisions are in compliance with laws, regulations, policies, plans, internal procedures and contracts. The internal control system in the bank is monitored by managers who should assess, with reasonable certainty, whether the system is reliable or whether it requires changes. The Internal Audit Dept. is the main component of the bank's internal control system. Its main task is to verify and assess the effectiveness and efficiency of the internal control system and of the risk management system. Each of the 7 branches of our bank has its own controller, who is responsible to the director of the branch. But controllers also cooperate with the Internal Audit Department (the branches inform internal audit about their annual plans, main findings and complaints, if any). Internal audit shares relevant parts of internal audit methodology with the controllers. Also, several departments in the Bank's Headquarters have their own controller.
Denmark	– Group Credit and Risk Control; – Group Compliance; – Group Internal Audit.
Finland (3 respondents) *Questionnaire 1:*	The Board of Directors sets the targets for and decides on the internal control system. It also assesses its efficiency and effectiveness with its sub-committee, the audit committee. Internal audit as an independent and professional activity is an instrument used by the board/audit committee to evaluate the quality of internal control. The executive management is responsible for organizing internal control under areas of responsibility all over the group, according to the instructions issued by the Board. The reporting lines for incidents, including procedures for annual reporting, are included in the internal audit system.
Questionnaire 2:	Internal control is the responsibility of each and every person, and more especially of those in management positions. In our banking group, we also have a special risk management function, whose task is to control and manage risks. Of course, the internal audit function is part of the control system.

Finland *Questionnaire 3:*	Internal controls in the Bank are an integral part of each employee's work. The heads of department and units (including the Management Committee) are responsible for internal control. Principals who lead and monitor their operations, and persons working in the monitoring, evaluation and quality control fields, are in practice most closely concerned by internal control matters. Furthermore, Internal Audit (IA) actively participates in maintaining and developing good internal control. In the last instance, the President and Chief Executive Officer and the Board of Directors are responsible for the organization's internal control. The Internal control system is organized at different levels: Operational staff, whether in front offices, middle offices, back offices or support functions, are the first employees to be involved in Permanent Control, in the form of first-level verifications. At a second stage, the corresponding management hierarchies, whose verifications take place either in the context of operational procedures, or of autonomous, control procedures, perform permanent, second-level verifications. Specialized functions, integrated autonomously into the operational organization of the Entities, or independent entities, make independent verifications of transactions. These are also part of permanent second-level verifications. Inspection Générale carries out independent periodic third-level verifications. Finally, the CEO is responsible for the organization of the Internal Control system and for all the information required by the banking law regarding the report on Internal Control. At least once a year, the CEO submits drafts of the reports relating to internal control and risks to the Board of directors for approval. The internal control and risks committee (operating as an audit committee) analyses not only the reports on internal control and on risk measurement and management, but the internal audit activity reports (periodic controls) and their main conclusions, including correspondence with the Banking Commission. It reviews the main orientations of the risk policy. It conducts hearings with the heads of Periodic Controls and Permanent Controls, deemed appropriate, and presents to the Board of Directors its views on the methods and procedures used. It expresses its opinion as to the organization of these functions within the Group and is kept informed of their work program. The organization of the internal control is described in the internal control charter.
Germany	The Internal Control System at HVB AG basically consists of three levels of control: – Operational controls (mainly Business Divisions); – Monitoring and supervision (Risk Management and Business Divisions); – Internal audit;

Italy	At Group level, a fourth, additional level of control exists: group internal audit. – Board of Directors; – Collegio Sindacale; – Internal Audit; – Head of Accounting and Control; – Risk management; – Compliance function.
Luxembourg	– Internal Audit: 4th level control => Audit & Compliance Committee. – Compliance: has responsibility at the group level (head office in Luxembourg and subsidiaries) for compliance to regulations. Implements 3rd level controls to assess that the controls are adequately in place in the Bank. – Compliance in our banking environment has a predominant role in regard to money laundering, investor protection, ethics, market abuses, anti-fraud controls and data protection. => matters are referred to the Audit & Compliance Committee. – Risk Management: • Operational risk: in charge of risk assessment in the Bank. Will be the coordinator of the updating of the risk matrix originally implemented by Internal Audit; • Risk management: in charge of market risk, liquidity risk, credit risk; – Organization: in charge of procedures in the bank. Guarantor of principles such as the 4 eyes principle of the segregation of duties (execution and control). – Other committees (including senior management level) : • Credit committee; • New product committee; • Asset and Liabilities committee; • Organization and Procedure committee; – Control entity over operational activities: nostri and securities reconciliation, control of confirmations...

Luxembourg	We identify first, a second and a third line of defence. First, line management must ensure that internal control is up to standards within their areas of responsibility. The second line of defence should ensure that the risks run by the bank are proportionate to the risk appetite deemed acceptable. This holds true for instance for credit risk, market risk and operational risk. Finally, internal audit takes a close look at whether the risks taken are well controlled. Internal audit provides the assurance to the management board and supervisory board that management is in control. Measures of improvement are being recommended to line management, whose duty it is has to take remedial action.
Poland	Internal controls are the significant measures of supervision and control of the banking activity. The objectives of internal controls are to assist the Bank's management in better achieving goals and in guaranteeing the safety and stability of the Bank's operations. Internal controls can be defined as: "a process, effected by Bank's Supervisory Board, Management Board, Management and other personnel, designed to provide a reasonable assurance regarding the achievement of objectives in the following categories: – Effective, efficient and secure business operations; – Safe custody of assets, both own and those entrusted; – Integrity, exclusivity and completeness of business and financial data and reporting; – Compliance to applicable laws and regulations including internal plans, procedures and general policies. The Bank's Supervisory Board and Management Board has the ultimate responsibility for ensuring that senior management establishes and maintains an adequate and effective system of internal controls, a measurement system for assessing the various risks affecting the bank's activities, and appropriate methods for monitoring compliance to laws, regulations, and supervisory and internal policies. The Supervisory Board supervises the implementation of the internal controls and assesses their adequacy and effectiveness. The Audit Committee monitors this on behalf of the Supervisory Board. The Management Board is responsible for designing, developing and implementing the internal controls that are suitable to the profile and level of risks connected with Bank's activity. The Management Board implements whatever measures are necessary to ensure that the Bank can permanently rely on a proper system of internal control and a Internal Audit function.

Poland	In this context, the Internal Audit Department is part of the ongoing process of monitoring internal controls, since it provides a reasonable, independent and objective assessment of the effectiveness and adequacy of the internal controls. This means that Internal Auditing is an independent consulting activity providing the objectively measurable assurance that value is added and the Bank's operations are improved. It helps Bank accomplish its objectives by bringing a systematic and disciplined approach to the evaluation and improvement of the effectiveness of the risk management, control, and governance processes.
Portugal	The internal control system in the Bank/Group is based on its governance model, which sets up a group of committees and commissions delegated powers by and answerable to the Board of Directors, aiming to keep a flexible organizational structure at Group level and a clear segregation of duties between business areas, operational areas and corporate (support) areas. Two of those commissions play a major role in terms of internal control: the Risk Commission, and the Audit, Security and Anti-Money Laundering Commission. Of the corporate units, the Compliance Office, Risk Office and Audit Division play a decisive intervention role in the internal control processes.
Slovenia	No reply
Sweden (2 respondents) *Questionnaire 1:*	– First line: Business operations; – Second line: Group Risk Control; – Third line: Internal Audit.
Questionnaire 2:	We operate three lines of defence. Management and the Board of Directors are the first line of defence against risk. It is the responsibility of the business management to identify, assess and manage risk, including establishing and monitoring a system of internal controls. Control functions, such as Risk Control and Compliance, form the second line of defence. They are responsible for establishing policies and frameworks which facilitate risk assessment and follow-up, as well as capturing items overlooked by management. We, Internal Audit, are the third line of defence. As an independent, activity designed to add value and improve the Bank's operations, by providing an assurance of objectivity, we help the Bank accomplish its objectives by bringing a systematic, disciplined approach to evaluating and improving the effectiveness of risk management, control and governance processes. We are not (and cannot be) responsible for performing the control duties of any business unit and/or control function within the Bank. However, we are responsible for evaluating how well the first and second line of defence perform their control duties. We are not a replacement for sound risk management practices.
Switzerland	Internal control is organized under Swiss Federal Banking Commission circular 06/6, which sets guidelines for corporate governance, the supervision of business and internal control.

Switzerland	Currently we have the three levels of control (lines of defence model, including integrated business processes, specific units ORM, IRM, Compliance...), and a third line of defence, which Internal audit. Two other lines of defence are included in the model, these being the external auditors and the regulators.
Turkey	Main actors are internal audit, internal control (including compliance), and risk management groups. Every division in a banking institution has a role to play under Turkish Banking Regulations.
UK / Ireland	Internal Control is based on the segregation of duties. We have a Risk Register and Risk Acceptance Register. These are monitored by an independent Risk Management function.

Question 4: How is internal audit organized?	
Belgium	Internal Audit is staffed by 12 employees. Four auditors perform agency in situ inspections, two are entirely dedicated to the review of Business Risk & Control Self-Assessment, one works on projects (MiFID, Leleux, etc), one is responsible for methodology, and another for the control of "shared entities". There are also lead auditors that are responsible for leading reviews (planning, audit program, testing, meetings, communications and audit report).
Bulgaria	The internal audit is a permanent function and operates as a separate department. The number of staff is approved by the Audit Committee or the Board. The internal audit performs an audit of each function in the Bank except for specific areas where it does not have the necessary expertise, i.e. the IT audit in smaller banks is performed as a co-sourcing engagement of external experts, or by the external auditors with the approval of the Audit Committee or the Board.
Czech Republic	The Internal Audit Dep. consists of three Sub-Departments: Operational Audit, IS/IT Audit and Audit of Risk management. There are 14 full-time staff (including a director and a secretary).The CAE is appointed by the Bank Board.
Denmark	As a mirror of the organization. Headed by a CAE.
Finland (3 respondents) Questionnaire 1:	Internal Audit organization is based on the main business areas (three units) and group services areas including Group IT (one unit). Additionally, risk control as a cooperative matrix interconnecting with the main base, forms one unit.
Questionnaire 2:	The Audit function has three departments: Internal Audit for the member banks, Internal Audit for the central institutions, and Security. There are also some internal auditors at our member banks.

Finland *Questionnaire 3:*	Internal audit is managed by an accountable internal auditor, who works administratively under the auspices of the CEO. But the Internal Audit Activity Plan is approved yearly by the Board of Directors. Internal Audit (IA) reports to the CEO, to the Control Committee and to the Board of Directors. The Internal Audit Department's staff consists of two full time internal auditors.
France	The work of the Inspection Générale breaks down into three large domains. The first domain involves a cross-departmental audit covering the whole function including: – Human resources and training, Finance, Mission Logistics; – Group risk Assessment, Group Consolidated Reporting and Planning, Incidents and Fraud; – Reference texts and Quality, Communication, Tools, Methodologies and Assignment Support. The second domain takes charge of specific risks at Group level, including: – Risks linked to market activities; models and actuarial audits; coordination of Inspection Générale actions in regard to the Basel 2 certification process; – Group IT Audit, including the Inspection Générale ICSI team; – Group Accounting Audit, including the Inspection Générale ECIC team. The third domain covers: – The heart of the customer/supplier relationship; – Responsibility for risk assessment and the definition and follow-up of the audit cycle in respective domains, as well as reporting on the findings of audit work; – Hierarchical responsibility for a group of Hubs, notably for managing staff, careers, resources and the budget process, which is submitted to the deputy head of function with responsibility for the budget. The domain manager is not directly involved in the performance of missions. IG functioning is a mixed system, relying on a pool of auditors and some specialized auditors.
Germany	Our Internal Audit is structured into seven departments, whose audits cover: – Retail and Corporate Division (two departments); – Markets & Investment Banking Division; – Risk Management & Control; – IT infrastructure & Applications; – Funds Transfer, Accounting, Human Resources, Budget Control, etc. The remaining department takes care of the internal organization, i.e. planning/control, IT support, data extraction, etc.

Germany	Decentralized audit units in London, New York, and Asia, among others, are assigned to the audit departments responsible for Markets & Investment Banking. Additionally, we have three regional offices for the audit of the domestic retail business.
Italy	Internal Audit is structured into: – Departments focused on business lines (postal/logistics, banking) and corporate processes; – Geographical area managers; – Dedicated staff services (planning & reporting, professional training, etc.).
Luxembourg	The Manager with responsibility for Internal Audit is in charge of the head office and subsidiaries, and takes part in the Audit Committee at the head office and in the subsidiaries. Two Managers are in charge of supervision in the head office and in the subsidiaries: – Local internal auditors report to them (all reports, action follow-up and quarterly reporting to the Executive Committee and Audit Committee); – The Managers have responsibility for reporting; – The Managers have responsibility for the audit plan; – The Managers have final oversight and responsibility for the performance of audit assignments; – 5 Senior auditors are in charge of the assignments at head office or in the subsidiaries; – 9 auditors.
Netherlands	The organization depends to a great extent on views of how its work can be performed effectively and efficiently. The set up of the internal organization required for internal audit may mirror the organizational structure of the bank itself, with departments primarily focusing on the different banking business lines and/or products. Increasingly teams are being formed to deal with specific banking risks, the assessment of which requires extensive expertise. This expertise is usefully combined into one department (for instance credit risk, compliance risk, market risk and ICT risk.
Poland	The Director of the Internal Audit Department also manages the IAD activity, due to the small size of the audit function and the number of auditors. The Director directly supervises the operations of the two teams: 1. Financial/operational auditors; 2. IT auditors.

Portugal	Internal Audit Division is organized into 8 Departments: Retail, Corporate Banking, Private Banking and Asset Management, Financial Markets, Operations, Accounting, IT and Employees. This organization reflects, with necessary adjustments, the model of organizational management and executive coordination in the Bank.
Slovenia	Under the Banking Act, the bank organizes its internal audit as an independent unit which is directly subordinated to the bank's management Board, and is ring-fenced from the other organizational units. The main actors involved in the internal audit are employees (at least one) who have acquired the title of auditor or certified internal auditor, under the Auditing Act. Those performing the tasks of internal auditing are debarred from other tasks within the bank.
Sweden (2 respondents) *Questionnaire 1:*	Country-based groups for administrative reporting – Cross-country teams to perform audit activity.
Questionnaire 2:	Globally. Local auditors at key locations. Staff assigned by business area. The Internal Audit Management Group – Core and Wider – directs the department.
Switzerland	We have a structure which matches our Group matrix organization, representing the different business lines and geographical zones.
Turkey	Internal audit is headed by a Chief Audit Executive. Internal audit has to audit all existing procedures within the banks including information systems.
UK / Ireland	Internal Audit is split into two teams: a business team and an IT team. However, there is a significant amount of collaboration between the teams.

Question 5: Is the Audit Function totally independent of the different operational entities?	
Belgium	Internal Audit is a totally independent function. The Head of Internal Audit reports directly to the Audit Committee, to the Head of Regional Control and to the CEO.
Bulgaria	The structural independence of Internal Audit is assured by the requirements set in a number of regulations, banning the CAE from taking other responsibilities within the bank. The Internal Audit Function is debarred from any operational responsibility over the business lines and other functions at the Bank.
Czech Republic	Yes, Internal Audit is functionally and organizationally independent of those audited. Its position is given by the organizational structure of the Bank, and reporting lines reflect IIA Standards.
Denmark	Yes, the Audit Function is totally independent.
Finland (3 respondents) Questionnaire 1:	The Internal Audit is totally independent from all entities of our bank.
Questionnaire 2:	The audit function is totally independent.
Questionnaire 3:	Yes!
France	According to professional standards, "Internal Audit provides an independent assurance of objectivity, and a consulting activity designed to add value and improve the organization's operations" in the words of the IIA standards. For the banking sector, the strict independence of the Periodic Control is imposed by the CRBF 97–02 article 7–2.
Germany	Yes, as required by MaRisk, Internal Audit is independent from the business and other operational functions of the organization.
Italy	It is totally independent from business and non-business functions.
Luxembourg	Audit function is totally independent.
Netherlands	In principle yes, because internal audit has to be able to come to an objective opinion that every part of the bank has taken adequate measures as far as internal control is concerned.
Poland	Yes, the lines of reporting support the independence of IAD.
Portugal	Audit Function is totally independent in relation to other functions within the Bank/Group.

Slovenia	Yes – it is separate from other organizational units in the bank. However, it is subordinated to the bank's management Board.
Sweden (2 respondents) *Questionnaire 1:*	Yes.
Questionnaire 2:	Yes.
Switzerland	Yes!
Turkey	Yes, internal audit is responsible to the Board (through AC or Member of the Board).
UK / Ireland	The Internal Audit function is independent of business functions.

Question 6: What is the reporting line of Internal Audit in the organization: linked to the CEO?	
Belgium	Internal Audit has three reporting lines: One to the Audit Committee (functional), one to the CEO (administrative) and a third to the Head of Regional Control (also functional).
Bulgaria	In most of the banks, Internal Audit reports to the Board of Directors through the Audit Committee. There is no current regulatory requirement for the establishment of an Audit Committee, although a number of banks have appointed one, as recognized best practice.
Czech Republic	All members of the Bank Board are informed after each audit engagement about main conclusions and recommendations of every audit. The CAE informs the CEO on a regular monthly basis about internal audit activity, results, potential problems etc. The Internal Audit Dept. informs the Board every half-year about its activity as whole and findings, and compiles a comprehensive report on an annual basis, on the results of its activity during the previous period. This report is submitted together with the plan for the following year to the Board for approval. It also includes a report on the fulfilment of those recommendations ensuing from previous audits and an appraisal of the risk management and internal control systems in the Bank. There is no Audit Committee in our bank.
Denmark	Reporting to the Board of Directors

Finland (3 respondents) *Questionnaire 1:*	The Internal Audit (GIA) is commissioned by the Board of Directors of our bank. It reports functionally to the Board and its sub-committee, the Audit Committee. The Board decides on the appointment and dismissal of Chief Audit Executive (CAE) of the GIA. The CAE reports administratively to the President of the bank.
Questionnaire 2:	The internal audit function reports to the Executive Chairman of the Board, and also to the audit committee and the board.
Questionnaire 3:	Internal Audit reports to the CEO, the Chairman of the Control Committee, the external professional auditors and to the accountable persons concerned. Furthermore, the Internal Audit every four months reports to the Board of Directors and the Control Committee the most important audit measures during the reporting period.
France	The Inspecteur Général reports to the Chief Executive Officer, who is kept informed of mission progress, as well as to the Board of Directors, either directly or through the Internal Control and Risks Committee. The Inspecteur Général is hierarchically responsible for all auditors. In specific cases, hierarchical supervision is delegated from the Group level to an appropriate person or management body, in accordance with regulatory constraints.
Germany	Following the two tier governance system usual for German joint-stock corporations, in our bank, Internal Audit is an instrument of the Board of Directors (Vorstand), but reports directly to the CEO, under whose authority it operates. Additionally, the Head of Internal Audit reports to the Audit Committee of the Supervisory Board (Aufsichtsrat) on a regular basis.
Italy	Internal Audit reports to the CEO.
Luxembourg	Internal audit is directly linked to the CEO of the Bank. All the internal audit reports are sent to the senior executives in charge of the activity.

Luxembourg	The Internal Audit reports, identifying and graduating important weaknesses, are reported to the quarterly Board of Directors. All the actions at a significant level of importance are followed up by the Executive Committee until they are implemented. Internal audit reports directly to the quarterly Audit & Compliance Committee.
Netherlands	The approach varies with each bank. The requirement is that Internal Audit takes an independent, objective position within the bank. Normally this is a position where the CAE reports to the CEO with a dotted line to the Audit Committee.
Poland	The internal audit has two reporting lines: – On a daily basis, it reports to the member of Management Board vested with the responsibility for Internal Audit (usually the Chief Executive Officer), and also – To the Supervisory Board: The Supervisory Board may appoint from among its members, the audit committee which supervises the activity of internal audit unit.
Portugal	Internal Audit Division reports directly to both the Executive Board and the Supervisory Board (Audit Committee). The Chief Audit Executive reports directly to the CEO and/or an Alternate Board Member, designated by the CEO.
Slovenia	In accordance with the Banking Act, the internal audit unit submits its half-yearly and yearly reports to the management and supervisory board. There is no special rule in the Banking Act for reporting to the audit committee of a bank.
Sweden (2 respondents) *Questionnaire 1:*	Board of Directors.
Questionnaire 2:	Direct reporting line to the Audit Committee and functional reporting line to the CEO.
Switzerland	In Switzerland, Internal Audit reports directly to the Board. However, we have a functional reporting line to the CEO. The above mentioned SFBC guidelines make an audit committee mandatory. Under the audit committee procedure, we have not only internal audits, but also reporting to the CFO, COO, ORM, IRM and Compliance units.

Turkey	Internal audit has to be independent, according to the regulations. Therefore internal audit reports directly to Audit Committee (AC is composed of at least two independent Board Members), or to an independent member of the Board.
UK / Ireland	The Head of Internal Audit reports directly to the chairman of the Audit Committee and has a dotted line to the CEO.

Question 7:
What is the scope of Internal Audit? Auditing of the efficiency of the permanent control? Advisory role? Regulatory controls?

Belgium	Within the scope of Internal Audit are all the activities performed by the bank, with a focus on assurance rather than on advisory activities and on operational rather than financial audits. Internal Audit is also responsible for quality review of RCSAs (Risk and Control Self-Assessment) and review of self-testing results (Self-testing being performed on a quarterly basis by all departments and sub-departments based on risks assessments). Finally, Internal Audit is involved in projects such as Basel II, MiFID, Leleux and other strategic/commercial projects within the bank (project monitoring and review).
Bulgaria	The focus of internal audit is assurance engagements, primarily operational engagements and compliance (to internal policies and regulatory requirements). Financial engagements are also performed but are still perceived as a duplication of the external auditors' work. The Regulation on internal controls in banks contains certain requirements about the scope of audit: - The application and effectiveness of risk management procedures and risk assessment methodologies; - The management and financial information systems, including the electronic information system; - The accuracy and reliability of the accounting records and financial reports; - The means of safeguarding assets; - The bank's system of assessing its capital in relation to its risk estimate; - Internal controls over transactions; - The effectiveness and results of internal banking operations; - The systems set up to ensure compliance to legal and regulatory; requirements, codes of conduct and the implementation of policies and procedures; - Compliance to agreements concluded; - The recruitment and qualification of personnel and compliance to delegated authority.

Bulgaria	The trend is to move to more involvement with consulting engagements. Sometimes these may be less formal engagements, than management requests "to take a look" before certain decisions or policies are implemented.
Czech Republic	According to the bank's Organization Chart, internal audit covers all activities, procedures and functions of the bank. The responsibilities of the Internal Audit Dept. are listed below: – Appraisal of whether controls are carried out so as to comprehensively cover the work procedures defined in the internal regulations; – Verifying and assessing the effectiveness and efficiency of the internal control system and the risk management system in the bank; – Monitoring, verifying and assessing of the bank's activities, operations, functions and systems in order to facilitate the prompt identification of risk; – Audits subject to the requirements and tasks of the Bank Board; – Co-operating with the external auditor, including the co-ordination of auditing activity; – Organizing initiatives on the part of the Public Protector of Rights; – Handling and investigating complaints. The Internal Audit Dept. also performs consulting engagements and provides expert opinion (particularly for IT systems projects). Internal audit undertakes regular risk assessment and maintains the Risk Map which is used for audit planning purposes. Internal auditor preventive consultancy/advisory services are being expanded.
Denmark	In Denmark the audit may be either financial and operational, or purely operational. Internal audits in Denmark are mainly financial audits. There are no special trends.
Finland (3 respondents) *Questionnaire 1:*	The scope is based on operational auditing to evaluate the bank's risk management, controls and governance processes with respect to: – The effectiveness and efficiency of operations; – Reliability and integrity of financial and operational information; – Safeguarding of asset; – Compliance to laws, regulations and contracts. The advisory role is at present determined by the independent role assigned to Internal Audit.

127

Finland *Questionnaire 1:*	Mandatory regulatory controls implemented annually are few in number, and mostly included in an annual risk assessment. In the questionnaire presented, areas such as compliance, BCP, Basel II, outsourced activities and MIFID, are good examples.
	What is the trend for keeping the role of independence as between different inside/outside stakeholders on different levels, when seeking to assure the quality of risk management, control and governance processes in a financial services group?
	– The trend is to recruit even more competent people and to improve processes based on the desired skills. Lore time and responsibility should be given to this, than it already is (rightly so), extending to consulting assignments, provided they are not damaging the role of internal audit. More information on other trends to serve stakeholders and to safeguard independence would be welcome.
Questionnaire 2:	The scope is as per the standards of the IIA. The trend is more consulting in the audit process; consultative auditing, not special assignments.
Questionnaire 3:	According to our Internal Audit Charter, internal auditing in the Bank is an independent activity based on objective assessments and consulting activity designed to provide the assurance that value is added and the Bank's operations are improved. It helps the organization to attain its objectives by bringing a systematic, disciplined approach to evaluate and improve the effectiveness of risk management, control and governance processes.
	The primary task of internal auditing is to analyze and evaluate the Bank's internal control systems, operational procedures and other systems. On the basis of observations, internal auditing formulates opinions and makes recommendations. The efficiency and reliability of individual operational processes and systems and compliance with statutes and other essential guidelines and regulations, constitute important elements in the area of responsibility for internal auditing.

France	The Inspection Générale intervenes independently in all the entities of the group and in all areas. Its scope therefore covers all activities and risks of Group's entities, including subsidiaries, financial or otherwise, within the scope of the auditors' remit, as well as all outsourced activities, in accordance with regulatory requirements.
	The Inspection Générale can raise any issue it deems necessary and has unlimited access to all documents, persons and property of the audited establishment.
	In past years, internal audit has driven missions to respond to statutory requirements, by undertaking advisory missions designed to provide an assurance of compliance.
	Audit assignments are threefold:
	– Verify the existence of framework written instructions and procedures for the BNP Paribas Group, verify the proper application of those written internal rules and procedures.
	– Verify that the Group internal rules and procedures are consistent with the regulatory requirements applicable to the Group.
	– Check the absence of major weaknesses in the internal control system and its consistency in all Group entities, as well as the reliability of the financial, operational and management data.
	The Advisory services are twofold:
	– Participation as an observer in meetings related to internal control;
	– Making contributions when requested to consulting missions (in this case, the same activity in the same entity may not be audited by the staff directly involved in the consulting mission).
Germany	The actual tasks of internal audit (as a periodical control function) are clearly segregated from permanent control activities. The role of Internal Audit is both to provide transparency and an assurance of sound practice to Management, and to provide consulting to the various lines of responsibility.
	As regulated by MaRisk, Internal Audit's primary task is to perform risk oriented „ex-post" audits on organizational units, processes, systems, products, models etc., as defined by the three yearly and annual audit planning. Specification of what is deemed of particular risk to the organization, is a responsibility of internal audit, but needs also to be assessed and documented for external review (by regulators, external auditors).
	„Ex-ante" activities, i.e., among other things, involvement in major projects as part of the project governance and supervision function, take up an increasing amount of Internal Audit's resources. This is deemed necessary by MaRisk in order to identify potential significant weaknesses before they materialize.

Germany	With the objective of providing added value to the organization, and its management, „Consulting" becomes a task increasingly relevant to the Internal Audit function. Its cross-functional approach, as well as its distinct understanding of the structure and behaviour of the organization and its Internal Control framework, enables Internal Audit to counsel all levels of the organization.
Italy	The trend for Internal Audit is that its mission covers both assurance services, relevant to internal control system assessment, and consulting services in respect to internal control system design and functioning.
Luxembourg	Internal audit not only checks that procedures are respected, but above all that risks are mitigated. All the activities of the bank have been mapped by Internal audit through a risk matrix that is ready for operational use in the context of Bale II.

After an acquisition, Senior Management asks Internal Audit to implement a detailed assessment of the subsidiaries, including setting up a risk matrix covering all the activities of the subsidiary and performing tests. Internal audit can be used by Senior Management to ensure that their decisions do not go against the internal control principles (reorganization of an activity for instance).
What is the trend?

Internal audit does not take part in project management, because Internal Audit must remain independent. However, if major projects are on-going (i.e. MiFID), the trend is to commission an audit assignment before the deadline for completion, for early warning of inappropriate orientations by Management. |
| Netherlands | Internal audit focuses on providing additional assurance that risks are managed effectively. Normally Internal Audit is expected to add value to the business by providing advice as a spin-off from its compliance assurance activities. For regulatory purposes, internal audit is expected to address issues such as compliance, Business Continuity, Basel II, Outsourced activities, Reliability and continuity of the ICT systems and MIFID.
What is the trend?

Senior management relies increasingly on the effective functioning of internal audit. To that end reviews are carried out to test whether internal audit is doing a good job. The trend is that internal audit tests whether (for instance) credit risk models have been constructed in a professional way. |

Poland	The primary objective of internal audit is to test and assess the adequacy and effectiveness of internal controls and also to express opinions (including risk management) with respect to management of the bank. IAD is also involved in consulting assignments (new procedures and policies) and also in pre-implementation audits.
	Audit priorities are set in the Annual Audit Plan. The basis for the developing the annual audit plan is risk assessment, which should determine significant areas and processes to review. Risk assessment identifies and considers either internal issues (such as change in the organizational structure, new products, new objectives and projects for the Bank, rotation staff and managers, new IT applications and systems), or external risks and issues (changes in economic environment, changes in competitor activities, technological progress, new laws and regulations), which may adversely affect meeting objectives set. The management should be involved in the process of annual audit planning, to ensure that the AAP is coherent with the Bank's objectives.
	What is the trend?
	As regulators have increasingly high expectations of IAD grow, it is more and more focused on testing compliance to local regulations (i.e. Basel II requirements).
Portugal	According to its Charter, the mission of the Audit Division is to contribute to meeting the targets set by the Bank/Group, and assuring its stakeholders – the Audit Committee and the Executive Board of Directors – of the efficiency and adequacy of internal control and risk management systems, and of the compliance to corporate rules and procedures.
	Within its normal course of work, the Audit Division may engage in consulting activities, involving providing services to the organization.
Slovenia	About the legally-prescribed scope of Internal Audit see the answer under the third question.
	On the other hand, the purpose, importance and tasks of the internal audit unit must be defined by a written document approved by the bank's management Board in agreement with the supervisory Board.
	Moreover, the bank's management Board in agreement with the supervisory Board is required to adopt an exact one-year plan of activities of the internal audit unit. That plan must include the following:
	1. Areas of operations subject to audit and,
	2. Specification of the content of planned reviews of operations by area.

Sweden (2 respondents) *Questionnaire 1:*	70 % Audit of efficiency in governance, risk management and controls, 20 % compliance/regulatory audits, 10% Advisory/Consulting. Though Regulatory requirements put pressure for increasing the resources allocated to mandatory regulatory controls, stake holder expectations are to increase added value by means of efficiency audits.
Questionnaire 2:	To provide reliable and valuable assurance to the Board and Executive Management in regard to the effectiveness of the controls, risk management and governance processes mitigating current and evolving high risks should be implemented, in so doing enhancing the control culture within the Bank.
Switzerland	We prepare a risk-based annual planning schedule, including regulatory requirements and assistance to our external auditors. Our audits adopt a risk-based approach to ensure that the first and second levels of control are working adequately and efficiently. What is the trend? To be less focussed than in the past on consulting and special investigations.
Turkey	In addition to compliance tests, internal audit performs consultancy activities, supplemented by audits of efficiency and effectiveness, but this specific role varies amongst banks. What is the trend? Greater role for consultancy and increasing involvement in Information Systems Audits.
UK / Ireland	Internal Audit covers all products, process and systems of the bank. These are reviewed on a 1 – 3 year cycle depending upon the inherent risk level. Internal Audit also undertakes project audits on an ongoing basis and is actively involved in projects such as MiFID and Basel 2. What is the trend? The trend is to increase the project management and advisory work.

Question 8: What specific skills and competencies should an auditor have?	
Belgium	Most importantly risk management and control technique focus. Internal Audit should have sufficient skills to cover all the Bank's businesses. Experience and IIA certifications are a plus.
Bulgaria	The auditor should have excellent communication skills and profound knowledge of the Bank's activity and services. The auditor should have fairly good knowledge and understanding of IT technologies and risks. The auditor is encouraged to obtain professional qualification such as the CIA.
Czech Republic	The Internal Audit Dept. is an all-graduate intake, supplemented by a range of audit-specific qualifications. CIA (IIA) and CISA (ISACA) certifications are supported. Auditors must exhibit requisite personal qualities and technical knowledge. Their skills are subject to on-going improvement initiatives: – Training appropriate to each auditor's duties; – Seminars (organized by the bank or by in the Czech Institute of Internal Auditors); – Foreign seminars in other central banks; – Familiarization with best practice when visiting other central banks or the ESCB Internal Auditors Committee; – Rotating auditors' duties. Auditors should have an ability to communicate effectively during audit assignments. Communication skills may therefore be developed in special seminars outside the bank.
Denmark	The Chief Internal Auditor must have at least Master's qualification in Auditing.
Finland (3 respondents) *Questionnaire 1:*	In addition to the personal qualities required by the audit, business and global environment, communication, analytical and IT skills are needed, as well some experience in one or more additional areas (finance, auditing, management, IT, laws and regulations, etc.). New recruitment should be made with the aim of bringing in new knowledge to specific areas of internal audit.
Questionnaire 2:	An auditor should fully understand our group's banking and insurance businesses. He/she should be familiar with economics, business administration, the law, ICT. An auditor should have a master's degree(M.Econ & BA or LL.M). An auditor should have good communication skills and at least one (if not more) foreign languages. An auditor should be conversant with audit processes, risk management, accounting systems, ICT, financial laws and regulations.

Finland Questionnaire 3:	Master's of Science in Economics, specialization in finance and accounting. Minimum of 3 years experience in professional internal or external auditing within a financial institution, or alternatively similar experience in other type of institution. Furthermore, the internal auditor should have skills acquired from experience in management/leadership, some IT experience/knowledge, ability to co-operate with different types and groups of people, analytical skills, integrity, listening skills, and oral/written communication skills.
France	Master's degree of Business, Economics or Engineer. Good English mandatory. The important skills for an auditor are: – Curiosity; – Ability to analyze and summarize; – Team spirit; – Ability to listen; – Strong communications skills; – Independence of mind; – Sound judgment; – Intellectual curiosity; – Certification (CIA, CISA, CCSA, CPA...) is an advantage in the audit environment.
Germany	Under recruitment guidelines, the specific skill of an internal auditor are: – Ability to work independently; – Ability to work effectively under pressure and tight deadlines; – Good project management and problem solving skills; – Accurate and quality focused; – Good presentation and communication skills; – High integrity and discretion.
Italy	Oral and written communication, process analysis, knowledge of applicable laws and regulation, IT audit competencies.

Luxembourg	To have good all-round knowledge and experience, yet have specialist skills. Note that being over-specialized can sometimes hinder raising the fundamentally simple questions which can be so revealing. Ability to synthesize and ability to adopt an overview, are valuable skills as the auditor has to deal with a mountain of information. Human contact must be in the equation at all times.
Netherlands	The auditor must have general audit expertise, but also sufficient business knowledge to be able to discuss business issues with line management. He/she should have good interview skills but also the ability to put findings in perspective.
Poland	The auditor should: – Have higher education qualifications (economy or law); – Have minimum 1 year auditing experience; – Possess strong analytical skills and be detail-oriented; – Be able to identify audit risks and assist in the development of testing procedures; – Possess good communication skills including the ability to verbally communicate with client personnel, as well as strong writing skills to prepare clear and concise narratives that highlight important controls; – Be able to independently carry out audit testing procedures within a budgeted time frame. Clearly and concisely summarize exceptions, reach conclusion on the effectiveness of the clients operating environment; – Possess good PC skills, and work on audits efficiently with various software applications (Windows Environment).
Portugal	Over and above the necessary technical skills inherent to the audit function, auditors should have good background knowledge, either generic (accounting, management, information systems, etc.), or specifically banking-related.
Slovenia	For tasks internal audit tasks, a bank must employ at least one person accredited under the Auditing Act as auditor or certified internal auditor, both licensed by the Slovenian Institute of Auditors. Minimum license requirements to obtain a license are: 1. University degree; 2. Minimum of two or five years' work experience (depending on type of license); 3. Examination of professional competence, qualifying for the tasks of certified internal auditor or auditor; 4. Absence of conviction for commercial or property crime with res judicata effect; 5. Knowledge of Slovenian language.

Sweden (2 respondents) Questionnaire 1:	General audit competence preferably combined with experience in one or more operational area (Financial instruments, IT, Lending etc.)
Questionnaire 2:	– Awareness of the IIA Professional Practices Framework, of concepts of COSO framework and international best practice – Team player with an open mindset working as an integral part of the audit team; – Excellent communication and interpersonal skills; – Commitment to personal development; – Analytical skills; – Accounting or banking background is an advantage.
Switzerland	– Ability to prioritize activities and to operate under the highest standards of ethics; – Good organizational and multi tasking skills; – Self motivated, resourceful, thorough, and capable of working under time pressure and meeting deadlines with minimal supervision; – Strong analytical skills; – Excellent interpersonal and diplomatic skills; – Confidentiality; – Written and verbal communication skills; – Computer literate; – Robust character; – Able to work in teams and alone when necessary; Professional and educational experience, either a university degree in economics or business or other qualification in finance or accounting, diploma in finance or accounting, 5 years work experience in banking. CIA or CPA mandatory.
Turkey	Good educational background; Competency at least in one foreign language; Computer literacy; Integrity; Ability and willingness to travel.
UK / Ireland	A variety of skills appropriate to the business. A detailed knowledge of banking products dealt by the Bank is important. All auditors to be professionally qualified with MIIA or PIIA or ACCA, etc. The ability to communicate well is also a key competency in an internal auditor.

Question 9:
Does the audit function represent an attractive career opportunity for a young executive? How would you describe the market trend for this position?

Belgium	Audit function (including external and internal audit) represents a great career opportunity for a young executive; it opens doors to management and Financial Control. With recent new regulations (i.e. SOX), recruiting skilled internal auditors has become very important. Also more and more auditors are certified (CIA, CISA, CCSA, CFE etc).
Bulgaria	In most of the banks the profession still has a negative (simply reporting errors and/or irregularities to senior management). The profession is mostly attractive in the financial institutions where the management has knowledge and understanding of internal audit. The "new type of auditor" is still a scarce resource and in demand on the market. The trend so far is career development within the internal audit profession rather than moving towards other executive positions.
Czech Republic	The importance of the audit function is growing in our country and is a good start to an executive career.
Denmark	At present, not attractive to any high degree.
Finland (3 respondents) *Questionnaire 1:*	The audit function represents an attractive opportunity for a young executive, if the function benefits her/his career. An awareness of the ambitions of each young auditor in each audit organisation is necessary, not only in countries/markets where there is real competition among competent people. The trend is to increasing competition among competent staff in this field.
Questionnaire 2:	A career as an internal auditor is today attractive. It is therefore relatively easy to hire qualified people, from junior to senior profiles.
Questionnaire 3:	Internal Auditing is still an attractive career opportunity for a young executive. The market has been growing and the trend is positive.
France	Often the audit is considered as a springboard for the young graduates, which makes the function attractive. Furthermore the transition period into a longer term career structure is often short (from eighteen months to three or five years). The work opportunities in this field are increasingly diversified, opening up broader professional vistas, with a possible international component. Experience acquired through practice is the best training in addition standard educational qualifications, making auditors very much sought after in the jobs market.

France	The demand for auditors is on a favourably rising trend for the profession, due to the increasing stringency of banking regulations.
Germany	Working with Internal Audit provides a good opportunity for young professionals to gain a general understanding of the institution, its governance, processes and controls.
	It offers a cross-functional perspective as well as a generalist and comprehensive approach. Reporting lines are straight to the organization's top management and executives, thus fostering a „management-minded" approach. It also improves awareness in the field of control, risk-reward calculations, etc., among other skills attributes valuable for young executives.
	There are examples in the past of internal auditors who, after 3-5 years of working with internal audit, took on managements (seat on Board of subsidiary).
	The market trend is positive due to organization increasingly needing control- governance-related jobs. The banking sector in particular requires more audit professionals.
Luxembourg	Thanks to their audit assignments and contact with management in the entities, internal auditors develop a global insight into the activity of the bank, how it functions, and what are its key interactions.
Netherlands	Internal audit normally serves as a pool for talent. The auditor has the opportunity to become familiar with the banking business. 5 years in audit prepares for the next step, often into the position of controller in one of the business lines. Auditors' attitudes are risk aware, which is helpful for setting up appropriate risk control in a bank. Auditors are also familiar with the details of the bank's workings.
	The market trend is that these career opportunities are increasing over time, due to the call for enhanced risk control.
Poland	The audit function represents an attractive career opportunity for lower or middle level managers.
Portugal	The increasing level of demand from the supervisory bodies, in regard to the adherence of Banks and other financial institutions to best practice in terms of governance, internal control and risk management, will lead to changes in the conventional role of the internal audit function in the organisation.
	The demand for the technical skills of auditors will tend to increase. Thus the banks' audit functions can add value to organisations by assisting management in accomplishing their objectives through improving the effectiveness of the governance, risk management and control processes.
	Internal audit may therefore be an attractive career opportunity for young executives.
Slovenia	No reply.

Sweden (2 respondents) Questionnaire 1:	In general attractiveness is satisfactory, and increasing in recent times.
Questionnaire 2:	The market trend for internal auditors differs, depending on location. Market demand is rising for new audit skills, due to new regulations and the increasing prevalence of cost saving drives within the Bank overall, which may hinder the effectiveness of internal controls. The quality assurance requirements imposed by the IIA further strengthen the demand for new staff.
Switzerland	I am of the opinion that internal auditor positions are very attractive. However, the market is not reflecting this trend, as newcomers are seeking employment in departments that generate profits.
Turkey	Yes, internal auditors perceive their role as challenging and rewarding. The general trend is that auditors transfer to other units of the bank after several years of duty in internal audit Department.
UK / Ireland	There is a clear career path out of internal audit into the business if an individual wants to take it. It is likely that not all junior auditors will want to make a career in internal audit, so it is important that it is seen to offer a route to business management positions.

Question 10: How is the audit function positioned in your organisation, regarding personal development?	
Belgium	Being part of an international group, our bank offers many career opportunities. The company offers local and group level internal audit positions. We also have peer reviews organised within the group. This offers many career opportunities abroad and locally. Working in audit is also considered a fine school of management. A background in audit can therefore be a serious advantage when applying for a new position.
Bulgaria	In the smaller banks, internal audit is viewed as a profession that requires specific skills and knowledge. The trend has been to move from a business function to internal audit. In certain cases the larger banks have the possibility to diversify and promote audit personnel to higher management positions within the organisation. But there is still little opportunity to use the audit profession as the stepping stone to an international career in the financial sector.
Czech Republic	The internal audit position is not yet perceived as a valuable career path, but there are many possibilities for individual development contributing to a career in and out of the directly employing bank, as well as for an internationally.
Denmark	Recently, internal audit has introduced successful young candidates to long term career jobs in the organization.
Finland (3 respondents) Questionnaire 1:	In internal audit as in any other function, there is a greater or lesser individual dimension to careers and development. Most internal auditors are recruited inside the bank, outside recruitment taking place if there are insufficient internal qualifications. After staying with us 3–7 years, the standard career path for the most qualified is a higher position in the bank in Finland or other countries. Another typical career path is in auditing itself: in different audit teams and areas, different countries and different positions in the bank or, in the consulting business or other services for external audit companies (big four).
Questionnaire 2:	It is possible to make a career as an internal auditor until retirement or move on to other positions (bank manager, controller, compliance officer, in-house lawyer etc.).
Questionnaire 3:	Internal audit has a high ranking in the organisation and the level of individual development is high.
France	Internal audit is a high ranking position, due to the global vision it affords of the bank's business. The position also fosters considerable personal development. Audit offers real career opportunities. After a short period in the Inspection Générale, auditors may access management posts.

Germany	Internal Audit is not deemed a compulsory or routine step in the individual development of young professionals in our bank, nor is it a privileged school of management or path for an international career as such. However, as stated under 9, on an individual basis, working in Internal Audit for a certain period may be the right choice for a young professional aiming at a management career.
Italy	Audit is a good professional opportunity to start an internal career path or to consolidate professional seniority.
Luxembourg	Turnover in the department is not high, because Internal audit is considered as a genuine „metier". Auditors are regularly required to move in the bank and access posts at management level.
Netherlands	Internal audit has the same status as other divisions within the bank, as far as individual development is concerned. Auditors are, like others, participants in courses to develop management talent, and have opportunities for international careers. Within the division, internal audit skills and the in-service training of auditors are matters of great importance.
Poland	As recent experience shows, the audit function is becoming a privileged management training school. In the last two years, auditors have been offered middle level management or independent positions in the organisation.
Portugal	Audit Division presents a diversity of situations, in terms of its staffing. A group of highly experienced professionals with several years in banking audit, coexists with significant staff turnover. Given the level of knowledge required of all areas of the Bank and/or wider Group, the Audit Division may well be considered a "privileged school of management", providing the skills and competencies that will be usefully applied when working in other areas of the Bank/Group.
Slovenia	No reply.
Sweden (2 respondents) *Questionnaire 1:*	In general there are three groups: 1. Young executives who spend a year or two "learning" how the group works, and establishing a top management network that should be useful when identifying future career opportunities in the bank. 2. Young executives (often from External Audit firms) who want to make a career within Internal Audit. 3. Senior executives who "end" their career in internal audit taking advantage of their operational experience and at the same time learning a new profession (Internal Audit).

Sweden Questionnaire 2:	GAM, which will be rolled out fully in 2008, sets a basic framework for personal development. Through the use of a common methodology, the internal audit function will be able to create perceived stakeholder value, raise the quality of work, ensure the effective use of resources and enhance skills development. The benefits, on both an individual and aggregate level, include among other things: – Alignment of global work practices; – Comprehensive planning, setting the priorities, scope and direction of audit work – Efficient execution; – Structure for knowledge management; – Training; – Supervision procedures; – Monitoring, QA and Benchmarking; – Communication. The quality assurance program to be rolled out in 2008 will allow internal audit Management to review and assess staff performance, as part of the annual individual staff assessment and remuneration process.
Switzerland	Skills development centre oriented on the development of competencies.
Turkey	A path to senior management, a necessary step for promotion. Not in big numbers in terms of international careers for the moment, but with the rapidly increasing presence of international banks in the market, international career opportunities are on the rise.
UK / Ireland	Internal Audit provides an excellent training ground for junior staff and this is recognized by Management.

Sources and Literature

On Regulatory Environment and Supervision

- Principles for home-host supervisory cooperation and allocation mechanisms in the context of AMA, Basel Committee, November 2007.

- Core Principles for Effective Banking Supervision, and Core Principles Methodology, Basel Committee, October 2006.

- Report on international Developments in Banking Supervision, Basel Committee, September 2006.

- High level principles for business continuity, Basel Committee, August 2006.

- Basel II International Convergence of Capital Measurement and Capital Standards, A revised framework, Basel Committee, June 2006.

- Home-host information sharing for effective Basel II implementation, Basel Committee, June 2006.

- Compliance and Compliance function in banks, Basel Committee, April 2005.

- Consolidated KYC Risk Management, Basel Committee, October 2004.

- Internal audit in banks and the supervisor's relationship with auditors, Basel Committee, August 2002.

- The relationships between banking supervisors and bank's external auditors, Basel Committee, January 2002.

- Customer due diligence for banks, Basel Committee, October 2001.

- European Union Banking Structures, ECB, 2007 and 2006.

- Procedure Lamfalussy, FBF, December 2007.

– Different articles from "Revue Banque" notably:
  - Article "Audit et gouvernance d'entreprise", September 2008.
  - Fiche de synthèse "Supervision bancaire & financière", FBF, juillet 2008.
  - Revue Banque n°702, dossier "Supervision Bancaire Européenne", May 2008.

On Internal Control and Auditing

– Enterprise Risk Management Framework, Committee of Sponsoring Organization of the Treadway Commission (COSO), September 2004.

– Internal Control Integrated Framework, Committee of Sponsoring Organization of the Treadway Commission (COSO), 1992.

– Definition of Internal Auditing, Code of Ethics and the International Standards for the Professional Practice of Internal Auditing, The IIA.

– Strengthening Governance in Banking sector, World bank review methodology, October 2007.

– OECD principles of Corporate Governance, OECD, 2004.

– ECIIA on Corporate Governance in Europe, ECIIA, April 2007.

– Top Seller: Audit Committee Effectiveness: What Works Best, 3rd Edition, IIA Research Foundation and prepared by PricewaterhouseCoopers, 2005.

– Audit Committee Handbook Fourth Edition, IIA, L. Braiotta, 2004.

– Common Body of knowledge CBOK, IIA, 2006.

– Théorie et pratique de l'audit interne, J. Renard, 2006.

– Position Paper on Internal Auditing in Europe, ECIIA, February 2005.

– Challenges in Government Auditing, IIA, 2004.

– 20 Questions Directors Should Ask About Internal Audit, IIA, J. Fraser, and H. Lindsay, 2004.

- Audit et Contrôle Interne Bancaire, A. Sardi, 2002.

- Internal Control and Internal Auditing, Guidance for Directors, Managers and Auditors, ECIIA, November 2000.

- Position Paper on the Internal Auditor's Role in the Prevention of Fraud, ECIIA, October 1999.

- L'audit interne vers une collaboration renforcée avec ses partenaires externes, IFACI, September 1998.

Webgraphy

Basel Committee
www.bis.org

CEBS
www.c-ebs.org

COSO
www.coso.org

ECB
www.ecb.int

EBC
www.ec.europa.eu

World Bank
www.worldbank.org

Beligium Banking Commission
www.cbfa.be

Bank of Bulgaria
www.bnb.bg

Czech National Bank
www.ourbank.cz

Danish Financial Supervisory Authority
www.dfsa.dk

Finn Financial Supervision Authority
www.rahoitustarkastus.fi

Commission Bancaire
www.banque-france.fr

Bundesamt für Finanzdienstleistungsaufsicht
www.bafin.de

CONSOB
www.consob.it

Banca d'Italia
www.bancaditalia.it

CSSF
www.cssf.lu

The Netherlands Authority for the Financial Markets
www.afm.nl

Bank of Poland
www.nbp.pl

Bank of Portugal
www.bportugal.pt

Bank of Slovenia
www.bsi.si

Finansinspection (Swedish FSA)
www.fi.se

Swiss Federal Banking Commission
www.ebk.admin.ch

Banking Regulation and Supervision Agency
www.bddk.org.tr

Financial Supervision Authority of the UK
www.fsa.gov.uk

IIA
www.theiia.org

ECIIA
www.eciia.org

IFACI
www.ifaci.com

FBF
www.fbf.fr

OECD
www.oecd.org

Glossary

Assurance Services – An objective examination of evidence for the purpose of providing an independent assessment on risk management, control, or governance processes for the Organization. Examples may include financial, performance, compliance, system security, and due diligence engagements.

Audit Committee – The Audit Committee of the Board of Directors assists the Board of Directors in fulfilling its responsibility for oversight.
The European 8th Directive on statutory audits of annual accounts and consolidated accounts indicates that *"Each public-interest entity shall have an audit committee. The Member State shall determine whether audit committees are to be composed of non-executive members of the administrative body and/or members of the supervisory body of the audited entity and/or members appointed by the general meeting of shareholders of the audited entity. At least one member of the audit committee shall be independent and shall have competence in accounting and/or auditing. The audit committee shall monitor the financial reporting process; monitor the effectiveness of the company's internal control, internal audit where applicable, and risk management systems; monitor the statutory audit of the annual and consolidated accounts; review and monitor the independence of the statutory auditor or audit firm, and in particular the provision of additional services to the audited entity"*.

Audit Function (also known as Periodic Control) – One of the two components of the internal control system which in some countries encompasses the "Inspection Générale" and Internal Audit.

Basel Committee – The Basel Committee on Banking Supervision is an institution created by the Central Bank Governors of the Group of Ten nations. It was created in 1974 and meets regularly four times a year. Its objective is to improve the quality of banking supervision by exchanging information on national supervisory issues, approaches and techniques and promoting common understanding. One of its last main works is the creation of a new frame related to the adequacy of the bank's Capital, as part of a series of recommended procedures known as Basel 2. It aims at replacing the Cooke (or Basel 1) ratio by the Mac Donough ratio, effective 01/01/2008. Basel 2 is supported by three Pillars (Pillar 1: Minimal Capital requirements, Pillar 2: Supervisory review process, Pillar 3: Market discipline).

Board – Variously known as Board of Directors, Supervisory Board, Head of Agency or Legislative Body, Board of Governors. The Board is by purpose in its various forms and irrespective of the names by which these are know, the governing body of an Organisation. It has the ultimate decision-making authority and, in general, is empowered to (1) set the company's policy, objectives, and overall direction, (2) adopt bylaws (also known as Statutes or Articles and Objects of Assoction (3) name members of the advisory, executive, finance, and other committees, (4) engage, monitor, evaluate, and dismiss the managing director and senior executives, (5) determine and pay the dividend, and (6) issue additional shares. Though all its members may not be engaged in the company's day-to-day operations, the entire Board is held liable (under the doctrine of collective responsibility) for the consequences of the firm's policies, actions, and failures to act.

CEBS – Committee of European Banking Supervisors (CEBS) is comprised of the Banking Supervisors and the Central Banks of the 27 European Union countries (namely Austria, Belgium, Bulgaria, Cyprus, Czech Republic, Denmark, Estonia, Finland, France, Germany, Greece, Hungary, Ireland, Italy, Latvia, Lithuania, Luxembourg, Malta, Netherlands, Poland, Portugal, Romania, Slovakia, Slovenia, Spain, Sweden and United Kingdom). The other countries of EEA (European Economic Area), Iceland, Liechtenstein and Norway, as well as the European Commission and ESCB (Banking Supervision Committee), are observers at meetings of CEBS. CEBS gives advice to the European Commission on banking policy issues and promotes cooperation and convergence of supervisory practice across the European Union. The Committee will also foster and review common implementation and consistent application of Community legislation.

CEIOPS – CEIOPS is the Committee of European Insurance and Occupational Pensions Supervisors. It was established under the terms of European Commission Decision 2004/6/EC of 5 November 2003 and is composed of high level representatives from the insurance and occupational pensions supervisory authorities of the European Union Member States. The authorities of the Member States of the European Economic Area also participate in CEIOPS.

CEO – Chief Executive Officer - responsible for an organisation's overall operations and performance. He or she is the leader of the organisation, serves as the main link between the Board of Directors (the Board) and the Organisation's various parts or levels, and is held solely responsible for the Organisation's success or failure. One of the major duties of a CEO is to maintain and implement corporate policy, as established by the Board. Also called President or managing director, he or she may also be the chairman (or chairperson) of the Board.

150

CESR – Independent Committee of European Securities Regulators. The Committee was established under the terms of the European Commission Decision of 6 June 2001 (2001/527/EC).

Charter – The charter of the internal audit activity is a formal written document that defines the activity's purpose, authority, and responsibility. The charter should (a) establish the position of the internal audit activity within the organization; (b) authorize access to records, personnel, and physical properties relevant to the performance of engagements; and (c) define the scope of internal audit activities.

Chief Audit Executive (CAE) – Top position within the organization responsible for internal audit activities. Normally, this would be the internal audit director. Other titles for this position are general auditor, chief internal auditor, and "inspecteur général". Generally, the CAE is the designated vis-à-vis of the National banking supervisor, and appointed by decision of the Board of Directors as responsible for ensuring the consistency and effectiveness of the Periodic Control assignments for the Organisation.

Comitology – More correctly known as "committee procedure". The term describes a process whereby the Commission, when implementing EU law, has to consult special advisory committees made up of experts from the EU countries.

Compliance – Conformity and adherence to laws, regulations, policies, procedures, contracts, plans, or other requirements.

Consulting Assignment – Advisory and related client services activities. The nature and scope of such assignments are agreed with the client. They are intended to add value and improve an organization's governance, risk management and control processes, without the internal auditor assuming management responsibility.

Control – Any action taken by management, the Board, and other parties to manage risk and increase the likelihood that established objectives and goals will be achieved. For the purposes of control, management plans, organizes and directs the performance of sufficient actions to provide z reasonable assurance that objectives and goals will be achieved.

COSO – Committee of Sponsoring Organizations of the Treadway Commission. This American committee drafted its work on "Internal Control – Integrated Framework" in 1992. The document was one of the most referenced internal control frameworks and Enterprise Risk Management procedures in 2006. It is sponsored and funded by five main professional accounting associations and institutes, the American Institute of Certified Public Accountants (AICPA), American

Accounting Association (AAA), Financial Executives Institute (FEI), The Institute of Internal Auditors (IIA) and The Institute of Management Accountants (IMA).

EBC – European Banking Committee – is the successor to the Banking Advisory Committee. It is run by the European Commission and generally meets three times a year. The Committee fulfils both comitology (q.v.) and advisory functions. It assists the Commission in adopting implementing measures for EU Directives and provides advice on policy issues related to banking activities. The EBC is composed of high level representatives from the Member States and is chaired by a representative of the Commission.

ECB – European Central Bank – is the central bank for Europe's single currency, the euro. The ECB's main task is to maintain the euro's purchasing power and thus price stability in the euro area.

ECOFIN – **The** Economic and Financial Affairs Council or the ECOFIN Council. This configuration of the Council of the European Union (EU) is composed of the Economics and Finance Ministers of the Member States, as well as of Budget Ministers when budgetary issues are discussed. As a configuration of the Council of the European Union, the ECOFIN Council has all the powers of the Council and follows the procedures specific to this body (Articles 202 to 210 of the foundation Treaty of the European Community). It meets once a month to deal with EU policy on economic and financial matters. The Presidency of the Council is organised on the basis of a half-yearly rotation system, whereby each Member State holds the Presidency for a period of six months.

EEA – The European Economic Area.

European Commission – The executive branch of the European Union.
The European Commission represents and upholds the interests of Europe as a whole. It is independent of national governments. It drafts proposals for new European laws, which it presents to the European Parliament and to the Council. It manages the day-to-day business of implementing EU policies and spending EU funds. The Commission also oversees that everyone abides by the European treaties and laws. It can act against rule-breakers, taking them to the Court of Justice if necessary.

European Parliament – Elected every five years by the people of Europe to represent their interests. The main job of Parliament is to pass European laws. It shares this responsibility with the Council of the European Union. It votes on proposals for new laws from the European Commission. Parliament has the power to dismiss the European Commission.

ESC – The European Securities Committee held its first meeting in September 2001. It is run by the European Commission and usually meets each month. It assists the Commission in adopting implementing measures for EU Directives and provides advice on policy issues in the securities field. As such, it fulfils both comity (the informal and voluntary recognition by the courts of one jurisdiction, of the laws and judicial decisions of another jurisdiction) and advisory functions.

ESCB – The European System of Central Bank is comprised of the European Central Bank (ECB) and the national central banks (NCBs) of all 27 European Union (EU) Member States.

External Auditor – An audit professional who performs an audit on the financial statements of a company, government, individual, or any other legal entity or organization, and who is independent of the entity audited. Users of the financial information of these entities, such as investors, government agencies and the general public, rely on the external auditor to present an unbiased and independent evaluation of such entities.

Four Eyes Principle – A security guideline that recommends that at least two people must witness or approve a particular activity. Organizations enforce this principle to protect themselves from dishonest individuals as well as from honest mistakes.

Fraud – Any illegal acts characterized by deceit, concealment or violation of trust. These acts are not dependent upon the application of threat of violence or of physical force. Frauds are perpetrated by parties and organizations to obtain money, property or services; to avoid payment or loss of services; or to secure personal or business advantage.

Governance – *"From a banking industry perspective, corporate governance involves the manner in which the business and affairs of banks are governed by their boards of directors and senior management, which affects how they set corporate objectives; operate the bank's business on a day-to-day basis; meet the obligation of accountability to their shareholders and take into account the interests of other recognised stakeholders, align corporate activities and behaviour with the expectation that banks will operate in a safe and sound manner, and in compliance with applicable laws and regulations and, protect the interests of depositors"* – Basel Committee definition – Enhancing Corporate Governance, February 2006.
"Corporate governance refers to the relationships between a business's management, its board of directors, its shareholders and other stakeholders. Corporate governance also determines the structure used to define a business's

objectives, together with the resources for achieving those objectives and monitoring the results obtained. Quality corporate governance should encourage the board of directors and management to pursue objectives which are in line with the interests of the company and its shareholders, and facilitate enhanced monitoring of the results obtained"– OCDE Principles of Corporate Governance, 2004.

Home Supervisor – A home supervisor is responsible for the oversight of a banking group on a consolidated basis. Host supervisors' knowledge of local market conditions can be an essential input into the home supervisor's assessment of the banking group. "Home – Host information sharing for effective Basel II implementation" – Basel Committee June 2006.

Host Supervisor – A host supervisor is legally responsible for the supervision of banking operations within its jurisdiction. Each host supervisor has a responsibility to provide information to the home supervisor for consolidated supervisory purposes. Conversely, host supervisors have a legitimate need to obtain relevant information – especially information related to a bank's risk profile and its ability to manage these risks – regarding the banking group that may have a significant impact on the subsidiary operating in its jurisdiction. "Home – Host information sharing for effective Basel II implementation" – Basel Committee June 2006.

Internal Auditing – also termed **Periodic Control** – is an independent, objective assurance and consulting activity designed to add value and improve an organization's operations. It helps the Organization accomplish its objectives by bringing a systematic, disciplined approach to evaluating and improving the effectiveness of risk management, control, and governance processes.

Internal Control – Process effected by an entity's board of directors, management and other personnel, designed to provide a reasonable assurance regarding the achievement of objectives in the following categories:
– Effectiveness and efficiency of operations
– Reliability of financial reporting
– Compliance with applicable laws and regulations
The most famous internal control framework is the COSO. In some countries, the Internal Control system encompasses Permanent and Periodic control.

Lamfalussy Procedure – The Lamfalussy procedure was established by the "wise persons" making up the Committee known as Lamfallusy, whose report of 15 February 2001, was concerned with the regulation of the European securities markets, subsequently extending in 2002 to the banking and insurance sectors. The procedure aims at accelerating the adoption of Banking Community texts, ensuring their appropriate implementation at national level.

National Banking Federation – An organization of National banking sector. The National Banking Federation is a forum where members' initiatives are proposed and debated. The NBF is a partner in dialogue with the National institutions in laying out the relevant legislation in the banking sphere.

National Central Bank – Ensures the smooth circulation of banknotes and coins, monitors the financial markets and oversees payment systems and media and, more generally, financial stability within the cost of a specific country.

Permanent Control – An overall system set up to permanently control risks and monitor the execution of strategic actions. It is based on policies, procedures, processes and control plans. These controls are carried out by different parties notably operating staff and their management and permanent control functions (Compliance, risk management, …).

QAR – Quality Assurance Review is a strategic assessment of the internal audit function including its infrastructure, staff experience, performance and its value added to the Organisation.

Risk – The possibility of an event occurring that will have an impact on the achievement of objectives. Risk is measured in terms of impact and likelihood.

Risk Management – A process to identify, assess, manage, and control potential events or situations, to provide a reasonable assurance regarding the achievement of the Organization's objectives.

Segregation of Duties (SoD) – alternatively called **separation of powers** – is one of the key concepts of internal control. It is a security principle which has as its primary objective the prevention of fraud and errors. This objective is achieved by disseminating the tasks and associated privileges for a specific business process among multiple users (for instance input and validation of a transfer by two different agents).

Standard – A professional pronouncement promulgated by the Internal Auditing Standards Board that delineates the requirements for performing a broad range of internal audit activities, and for evaluating internal audit performance.

World Bank – An internationally supported bank that provides financial and technical assistance to developing countries for development programs (i.e. bridges, roads, schools, etc.) with the stated goal of reducing poverty. It is not a bank in the usual sense. It is made up of two unique development institutions owned by 185 member countries – the International Bank for Reconstruction and Development (IBRD) and the International Development Association (IDA).